# The Cycle of Corruption

*To Dr Beague
Thanks for your support
from M.R. Irepo*

# THE CYCLE OF CORRUPTION

## THE DETERIORATION OF AN AFRICAN CITY

BY

**M.R. IREPO**

Copyright © 2012 by M.R. Irepo.

Library of Congress Control Number: 2011917912
ISBN:  Hardcover  978-1-4653-7583-4
       Softcover  978-1-4653-7582-7
       E-book     978-1-4653-7584-1

All rights reserved. No part of this book may be reproduced or transmitted in any form or by any means, electronic or mechanical, including photocopying, recording, or by any information storage and retrieval system, without permission in writing from the copyright owner.

REVIEWER: Professor Edward Cox-Rice University Houston, Texas USA.

This book was printed in the United States of America.

To order additional copies of this book, contact:
Xlibris Corporation
1-888-795-4274
www.Xlibris.com
Orders@Xlibris.com
103525

# TABLE OF CONTENTS

I. INTRODUCTION
   A. Dedication .................................................................... xi
   B. Why I Wrote the Book ............................................. xiii
   C. Preface ........................................................................ xv
   D. Acknowledgements .................................................. xvii
   E. About the Author ..................................................... xix
   F. Introduction of Goldteeth ........................................ xxi

II. STORY BEGINNING
   A. Irepo's Chronicle ........................................................ 3
   B. A Conversation with a Friend Nicknamed Goldteeth ... 5

III. HUMAN ENVIRONMENT
   A. Confrontation with the Lawyer ................................ 13
   B. Hospital Aspect ........................................................ 13
   C. Dug-Hole Well ......................................................... 19
   D. The Poor Are Not Close to the Rich ........................ 21
   E. Eating in Unsanitary Places ...................................... 23
   F. Gangsters' Role during Election Time ...................... 27
   G. Urinating on the Street ............................................ 29
   H. Office Messenger Environment on the Street and at Work ... 31
   I. Cultural Activities ..................................................... 33
   J. Mildew on Houses ................................................... 37
   K. Corruption in Excessive Practice .............................. 39
   L. Driving Confusion ................................................... 41
   M. Direct and Indirect Stealing .................................... 45
   N. Critique of Newspapers on Corruption .................... 47

IV. ECONOMIC ENVIRONMENT
    A. Labor Surplus ......................................................................... 53
    B. Product Availability ............................................................... 55
    C. Iron Steel Rods on the Sidewalk ......................................... 57
    D. Tourism .................................................................................... 59
    E. The Invisible Economy ......................................................... 61
    F. Live-stock on Streets and Roads ......................................... 65
    G. Marketing Place ..................................................................... 67
    H. Banking .................................................................................... 69
    I. Selling Medications ............................................................... 73
    J. Pilfering .................................................................................... 75
    K. Retirement .............................................................................. 77
    L. Disorderly Economic Development .................................. 81
    M. Distributing Goods and Services ........................................ 83
    N. Petrol ........................................................................................ 85
    O. Dwelling Place ....................................................................... 87
    P. Corruption Practice Part I. ................................................... 89
    Q. Corruption Practice Part II .................................................. 93
    R. Corruption Spreading Rampantly ...................................... 95

V. WORKING ENVIRONMENT
    A. Filthy Workplace ................................................................. 101
    B. Office Setting ........................................................................ 103
    C. Work Pressure ...................................................................... 107
    D. Ethics ...................................................................................... 109
    E. Tardiness and Favoritism at Work ................................... 111
    F. Making Job Valueless ......................................................... 113
    G. Cleaning of Gutter .............................................................. 115

VI. INFRASTRUCTURE ENVIRONMENT
    A. Parking ................................................................................... 119
    B. In Elementary School ......................................................... 123
    C. Bumpy Street and Road ..................................................... 125
    D. Power Plant Problem .......................................................... 127
    E. Transportation Alternative ................................................ 129
    F. Public Library ....................................................................... 131
    G. Murila International Airport ............................................. 133
    H. Shanty House ....................................................................... 135
    I. Traffic Lights and Toll Booths .......................................... 137

VII. SOCIAL ENVIRONMENT
- A. Family Burden .................................................................. 141
- B. Scary Night ...................................................................... 145
- C. Family Disassociation ..................................................... 147
- D. Track and Field Events.................................................... 149
- E. Entertainment ................................................................. 151
- F. Community ...................................................................... 155
- G. Familiarity Falls Apart.................................................... 159
- H. Which Politician Is Right or Wrong?........................... 161

VIII. DEMOGRAPHIC ENVIRONMENT
- A. Area Population .............................................................. 165
- B. IFA Belief......................................................................... 169
- C. Cultural Beliefs ............................................................... 171
- D. Habitual Practice............................................................. 173
- E. Marriage and the Baby Boom ........................................ 175
- F. Greeting ............................................................................ 179

IX. GEOGRAPHIC ENVIRONMENT
- A. City Appearance ............................................................. 183
- B. City Conditions............................................................... 185
- C. Census Time .................................................................... 187
- D. Pollution........................................................................... 189
- E. Lack of Fresh Air ............................................................ 191
- F. The Islands with the Biggest Island .............................. 195

X. SUGGESTIONS................................................................... 199

XI. CONCLUSION..................................................................... 203

# INTRODUCTION

# DEDICATION

This book is dedicated to the young generation and the old generation; the ones with vision and aspirations; and to individuals with genuine conviction. It is for those who can stimulate a quick, lasting revitalization of the City of Paradise, before the city is further relegated to an uncontrollable and unbearable place to reside in this 21st century. I hope the young people can get together with some of the older leaders and towns people to change the destiny of Paradise- before it completely destroys itself.

# WHY I WROTE THE BOOK

Although I was not a fast reader for a while, I enjoyed reading novels and magazines. I still do. Despite not being able to read fast, I continuously read. Then the thought of writing a book came into my head. I said to myself, "One day I will produce a book."

As time went by, occasionally, different topics sporadically crossed my mind. But, I constantly got stuck on how to develop them. Nevertheless, I did not give up on the idea. Then, when I was not even thinking about writing a book, while on an undertaking to purchase investment property for my family, I stumbled upon a compelling real life story – actually traumatic circumstances.

It has been many years since I had last visited Paradise City. At the time Paradise was the capital of Hope. It was in 1998, after I had sojourned in the United States of America for over 30 years, that I finally went back to visit my country, Hope, and saw again, this beautiful place – Paradise city.

Now years later, in 2007, I had decided to buy and build a home there. My number one reason: I was born on the continent of Africa, and Hope is my country. And, as a child I looked up to the City of Paradise. It was a beautiful, bustling place of prosperity, tourism and the middle class, a place where I lived well. The second reason was the Nira, compared to the American dollar, was only one third – a drastic difference.

Upon arriving in Paradise, many health hazards caught my eye and my senses. With the bombardment of filthy smells emanating from all over the majority of the streets of Paradise and the health barriers I witnessed with my own eyes (and the knowledge that this was happening all over in many other cities and towns), my aim of writing a book on "The Cycle of Corruption" became no longer a procrastination on my part. It became an absolute necessity.

Thus, I have written this book. Although a non-fiction entity, the book is a detailed description of the souring events in the City of Paradise. The story is told through my eyes: I am Irepo, the protagonist, as I narrate the events and through banter between myself and Goldteeth, my cohort and old friend who has lived in Paradise all of his life. Goldteeth is so named because of the one gold cap he got many years ago when he really had money. The name might also seem appropriate now because of the all yellow teeth he has in his mouth.

# PREFACE

The content of this book, Cycle of corruption, focuses on the deterioration of The City of Paradise, Hope, a fictitious country spurning from the chance travels of Irepo - the narrator. Irepo accidentally stumbles upon many problems throughout the City of Paradise while he is there on personal business. Though a novice, his point of view is quite profound. He comes to Paradise to build a house, but notices many drastic differences in the city's makeup and culture, since the last time he was there many years ago.

While there, he summons lawyers, contractors and the like to erect the house and decides to look up an old family friend, Goldteeth to tour the city with him. Irepo's keen observance of the city's surroundings, infrastructure, features, natural environment, and of course the populace, leads him to take a deeper look at their relationships and interactions.

As Irepo chums along with Goldteeth, his curiosity about the state of Paradise provides insight into how greed and corruption can take over any city in the world. This story of corruption takes on a life of its own through a probing eye. Irepo is a man intent only on building a house, yet this story asks so many of life's daily questions. Pages after pages of this book appeal to the senses of the everyday man and woman. As Irepo navigates through the necessary routines of building a house, and is confronted with so much negativity, he is constantly wondering and asking out loud, "Is there a better way?" As he seeks the answers, the reader, who may also want his 'piece of the pie', will get some insights into the answers, too.

Irepo questions the marked decline of the city from how it used to be to how it is at present. This profile of the Paradise city embraces a verbal discussion with its people, the strangers and the ones he knows – workers, friends, acquaintances and family members.

# ACKNOWLEDGEMENTS

Thanks to Emmanuel Olayiwola Babatunde for sharing with me the adverse effects of the widespread corruption on the everyday citizens in the City of Paradise.

I extend my sincere thanks to Olujimi Holloway for introducing to me, a dedicated editor for the book.

Without any hesitation, I am very grateful to Priestess May, a Spiritual Sound Healer and a magnificent writer who inspired me on putting the manuscript together.

Above all, I appreciate so much my beautiful wife, B.B for her support. Also, I want to thank her children C and K for allowing me to write without interruption.

# ABOUT THE AUTHOR

Irepo was born in the country of Hope. He finished high school in Fidee, and taught in an elementary school there. He later worked in Paradise City, the Ministry of Works and Survey for four years, before leaving for France in 1967. In 1968 he moved to the USA where he enrolled in the RCA (Radio Corporation of America) School, a technical trade school in New York City. He later gained admission to Pace University in 1970, where he received a Bachelor of Business Administration in 1973. Irepo has a dual Masters Degree from Long Island University (Brooklyn Campus), in business Administration 1974, Economics from Fordham University (Bronx Campus), in 1985.

He worked for the Health and Hospitals Corporation (HHC) at the head office as an Assistant Systems Analyst in New York City, before being transferred to the Harlem Hospital Center as a Systems Analyst. He later became Coordinating Manager. But, due to the recent budget crisis, he left to work for the NYC Taxi and Limousine Commission as an Administrative Staff Analyst. He retired in October of 2009.

# INTRODUCTION OF GOLDTEETH

Goldteeth is an old family friend. Although we were never close, I always admired his ways. He was always good mannered and did not get in much trouble when we were young. He is just one of those people who, despite limited introduction with him while growing up for some reason - you feel close to and have admiration for.

For whatever reasons, Goldteeth waited until he was in his forties to marry. He and his wife have a teenage son. He's always murmuring and complaining about his predicament of his financial problems. He is consumed with concern about how he is going to feed his family and pay his rent.

I try to reassure him by telling him not to worry too much. I always give him money when I see him, yet he still worries. As Goldteeth follows me around, he actually is keeping me company. He has no idea of the observations that I am making about the condition of the City of Paradise. He really is helping me to understand what I am looking at.

From what he is telling me, Goldteeth's expenses are astronomical. It seems no matter what I give him, the amount cannot be enough for him to support his household. The more I hang out with him, the more I realize the impact of corruption on his everyday life. This understanding is one of the major reasons why I compensate him so generously when he goes home at the end of the day.

# STORY BEGINNING

# STORY BEGINNING

## IREPO'S CHRONICLE

I am Irepo. My name means "friendship" in Yoruba, one of the primary languages of the country of Hope. My recent visit to the city of Paradise, in the country of Hope, on the continent of Africa, was on a Monday in May of 2007. I sojourned to Paradise City to build a house. The property there would be of great value to my family one day. I know that my American dollar would go far when compared to the Nira, our own country's currency. I wanted a house for income property for now and perhaps a home for retirement later.

I had made plans to meet a lawyer named Joyee Kuya. He met me at Murila International Airport. We went over all of the particulars that would enable me to build on this property and to get the requisite Certificate of Occupancy (COO). I told Attorney Kuya – I had only five days to get everything going; and that although I had to rush back to the states on a personal matter, I would be back in 2 months. Kuya told me not to worry about anything as he would take care of all that needed to be done on my second day he introduced me to a contractor, Kalim Sabu. Kalim and I talked for two and a half hours. I subsequently made an appointment to meet with Kalim on Thursday.

I realized I would have only a day to see the City of Paradise before getting together again with my now 'business' partners. The city had changed so drastically that on the third day after my arrival - I decided to take a mini tour to see what changes had occurred.

On the fourth day I was back to business. Kalim Sabu gave me an architectural rendering of the house that I wanted to build. It was beautiful! He captured all my ideas on paper. When I met with my attorney on Friday, my fifth and final day, Attorney Kuya told me, "By the time you get back in sixty days, the building will be in full swing, and the Certificate of Occupancy will be well on its way to being in your hands. We'll just be waiting for you to come back to sign the documents drawn up by the Land Reacquisition Unit". I gave him the money that he requested, plus a few extra dollars as a contingency (really KOLA, bribery money for all the would-be hustlers, the under the table dealers). That I thought would assure the work being completed without unnecessary delays.

# STORY BEGINNING

## A CONVERSATION WITH A FRIEND NICKNAMED GOLDTEETH

Though I had come to my beloved City of paradise to build a home, I also wanted to tour the city as well. Because the city looked so different and many changes had occurred, I could not do it alone. So, I called on an old friend of the family, (whom friends nicknamed "Goldteeth"), who still lives in Paradise City.

When he arrived, I peered deeply into his eyes because I could not recognize him right away. Although he is only in his late fifties, his appearance was like a seventy-year old man. After a few seconds, he started calling my name - and mentioning things that we both used to do together in the early days. I was amazed that he still possessed a photographic brain to remember the old events. It is these old memories that he was enumerating that pushed my memories back to those times, and which made me recognize him. This encouraged me to get closer to him.

His English is broken. He leaves out the articles many times. But as I listen to him speaking, I realize that I too sometimes do the same thing in my speech even though I have a masters' degree from the States. This is how we speak among family and old chums. It is okay. It is warm. It is home.

Immediately, we both hugged. Thirty years have elapsed since we've seen each other. Then, as we are still hugging, he squeezed me hard, like he was squeezing an orange to coring the last amount of juice out of it. He was so excited to see me that next he pumps my hand so hard it begins to hurt! So, I quickly bend down as if I am about to pick up something (invisible though it may be) and therefore let go of my hand that he stopped. I am relieved to say the gesture worked ending the dance of hugging and shaking of hands.

The following day we set out to tour the paradise city area. On our way, I asked him, "Why is it that there are so many people in Paradise? What is the cause of the overcrowding?"

He smiled and opened his mouth laughing with excitement. I laughed too. But, then, seeing only five teeth in his mouth, my smile quickly disappears. Seeing the look of horror on my face he explains, "My friend, there are not many dentists around, and they are so expensive. Besides, there is no money to pay the dentist". He added that he is not used to brushing his teeth at least twice daily. The only 5 teeth that he has are extremely deteriorated and decayed. "They are about to fall out." He confirms.

What is even worse, his bad breath hits me whenever he talks. It is like the smell of rotting fish that rises up like steam from boiling water - and suddenly engulfs you when the lid is taken off the pot. I was faced with a dilemma" of whether to endure being close to him when talking or use my handkerchief to cover my nose, in the process trying to make it look as if the bad breath that I smell is actually coming from somewhere else. I am truly in a quandary.

My final device is to constantly spray the deodorant that I carry with me since the city is also filthy, and the wind blows an intermittent unpleasant smell in our direction. As a result, whenever I spray, he seems to be refreshed. As he inhales the odor of the spray, this caused him to break out with a smile on his face. Soon - he gets closer to me.

"Are you not tired of smiling?" I asked. "No", he says. At least he does not suspect me of trying to get rid of his bad breath.

Going back to the questions I posed to him earlier about the city's deplorable condition, Goldteeth started smiling and talking, "Well, Paradise used to be the capital of Hope, before Idera became the new capital. At that time, there were many industries and the search for employment was no hustle". That is, it wasn't hard to find a job; it was very easy to find a good one. "At least then, both the blue and white collars felt happy and enjoyed their life. And, dirtiness was minimized."

I stressed, "I remember when Paradise used to be clean, not overcrowded." I went on about the dwellers and how they planned ahead before they relocated. But now only a few industries, which are competitive, remain. Now suffering is very obvious: There are fewer jobs. "There are too many paupers and beggars in the city!" I declared.

Goldteeth intervenes, "Different tribes are all over the nation. They migrate here with the hope of getting a job of substance." "However, one thing about the migrants is that they do not carefully plan the pros and cons of migration. They just get ready and go."

His statement makes me ask him about the accommodation problem, since all the immigrants do not have families who reside in the city. He patted me on the back and looked in my face as if to tell me I do not know what I am talking about. "In an open area which is not too close to the main roads, the Paradise City Council does not put up 'No Trespassing Signs'. The Squatters, therefore, go and occupy this area. They make tents and use them as their sleeping abodes, at least temporarily. And of course, under the open spaces of any bridge, the paupers use those areas as sleeping spots, also." I laughed as he said that with a vision of squatters sleeping everywhere.

He continues, "Nevertheless those who have relatives in the city are accommodated." He went on about how their hosting relatives do not mind accommodating the migrants even when they sleep in the same room or parlor, which is now stuffed with the migrant's luggage and other household items. The idea of accommodations is two-fold. It provides a space for sleeping in the night' and it also does not allow a relative to become a squatter, someone who hangs around the house all day, not looking for employment. It would be an immense disgrace to the relatives if any one of their families turns out to be a squatter. Squatting becomes a stigma that stays with the families for the rest of their lives. It is deemed in Paradise society as a failure by the host family, if they cannot provide accommodations for their own relatives.

I am astonished by what he is narrating. So I ask him: "How about the children? Do they have to sleep in the same room or parlor with their families? How would they be attended to?"

He responds, "The children are always patted to manage with their parents until a space is available. A space may be availed to them for a little bit more comfort only if some of the family members have stepped out for a while." If the children need to sleep when an elder is already in the space, the children must show respect and wait until the elder wakes up and leaves before acquiring the spot. Our children are always taught to give respect to the elders.

"Oh no, that is horrendous to hear!" I exclaimed. "And why do such relatives or parents prefer suffering rather than comforting?"

Instead of a direct answer to my question, Goldteeth vehemently puts me into an old memory again, saying, "The dwellers used to endure suffering beyond the limit. This behavior has always been typical and it still is part of the daily route." I recalled how it was before I moved oversees. Goldteeth's words had reminded me - that this behavior is still predominant.

"This is a matter of survival", he said. "Everyone is trying to maintain his or herself. There is no quick alternative avenue, unless a person has money to spend." And I quickly got it -. It was a tradition – to help a family member to have a place to stay, no matter how crude the surroundings, was thought of as help. A family obligation – to do otherwise would be disgraceful.

Looking around the city, I voiced my concern about the condition of the people as it stands today, "In the days before and after Hope's independence, males and females in the household obeyed the rules of good hygiene. They cleaned their teeth frequently, making them ready to smile more. They looked according to their individual age or even more youthful."

He replied, "People who were not lazy found a job and earned money to maintain them-selves. They showed a lot of pride in wearing clean clothes! Today people have to be extremely careful not to dress flamboyantly because there are many thieves." "There are so many people who are hungry, who are ready to sneak and rob you without any penitence. People cannot go out and stay late nowadays", he concluded.

"To piggy-back on your explanation," I interrupted, "I remember when the city of Paradise used to be clean and less densely populated. At that time, people looked healthier than today." I couldn't get over the shock, so I went on and on about how their way of living was about the subsistence level of today; how today the people looked fragile and old. I expressed my shock to see so many sick and poor. I was so hurt and disgusted at the same time to see what happened to my people, the way they live, their poor health and their lack of pride. I blurted out, "And there are panhandlers all over the city!"

We talked further about how Paradise City is less attractive since it lost its status as the capital to Idera. Neither the visitors - nor the tourists are impressed with how the city looks today. The ambiance is gone, so is the excitement, no longer clean or beautiful. No more attractions. It is obnoxious! Whatever few attractions there are now, no tourist wants to stay for the meager enjoyment the city offers. I said critically, "Paradise City has a 'see it quickly and then get out' atmosphere.

A person who is walking leisurely for half a mile along any street will not see Europeans shopping as they used to. The only location where they may be spotted is at the airport, when they are in transit, coming into or leaving the country. It's not that there aren't any Europeans in various locales -. It's just that - their population in the city has tremendously diminished compared to when Paradise was the capital of Hope. I have memories of driving along with the traffic and seeing many more Europeans. Although Europeans do still like Hope, they are now scattered all over the nation - as opposed to being concentrated in Paradise as was previously the case.

Today, Paradise city is full of indigenous people and migrants from neighboring countries. The migrants come believing there are available jobs. But the belief soon turns into a fallacy. The people become desperate and unruly. This makes the city more disorderly and vile. Many people become homeless – and eventually turn into beggars, hustlers and hecklers who cannot be controlled or wiped out from the streets. It's better to leave them alone, as they are seeking for their daily bread.

The law enforcement officers, who are trying desperately to reduce the high crime rate of scofflaws, hoodlums and robbers in the streets, have a hard way to go. With the lack of good equipment and supplies, the police cannot do their job properly. In addition, the administration is negligent in paying the police officers an adequate salary, causing the police and the auxiliaries to connive and scheme - rather than prevent a crime or robbery. They are always on the take.

Then, there are robbers, who are armed and dangerous. They attack innocent people! They take hostages! If their demands are not met, they kill people!!! Thus, people are afraid to be out late at night. As a result, decent people have a very limited amount of time for enjoyment and entertainment in the out of doors.

The poor children have no decent, clean place to play. The play grounds are not the way they used to be. School boys and girls have to create their own playground. Many of the old playgrounds have been converted into shopping centers. As a result, children have to be careful where they play - because violence seems inevitable. Whenever they cross streets to get to the other neighborhood playgrounds, there always seems to be some sort of danger. Other forms of recreation seem to be nonexistent. Recreation such as, "Regatta" seems to be extinct. Nobody is keeping it alive. Because of our proximity to the Atlantic Ocean, we devised many games for both fun and skill. Regatta taught us both skills. Team Work! It's something that was passed down through the generations.

Then, there is the issue of the quality and availability of drinking water. The lagoon which surrounds the city is not clean anymore. It used to be properly maintained, but no more. Therefore, the water is dirty and polluted, and not suitable for human consumption.

Everything I am observing is just infuriating. There is this yellowish dust, mingled in the air, which is unavoidable; and no matter what or where you are, you can't escape inhaling it. Many drivers have no air-conditioning. People who are walking and wearing light colored or white clothing must know in advance which streets to avoid – so that their attire does not turn dirty - like an instant tarnish.

The police are not around to direct traffic. The few traffic lights still standing are not functioning properly. The control of the traffic flow is in the hands of the drivers. And the driver who gets the first opportunity to go - will drive through the cross streets without yielding the right of way – especially since there is no one to police them. Because there are so many reckless drivers who prefer to disobey the law, pedestrians must be very careful crossing the streets and constantly watch out for vehicles and them-selves. In addition, many drivers who transporting people to their respective destinations during rush hours are hustling for passengers. Pedestrians are especially wary of them as they drive fast and reckless.

Bribery has become a way of life, and is very common among the Paradise city dwellers. It is unbelievable! Corruption of the politicians and the elites is disseminating down to the decent people who want to stay far away from the ones who prefer to do things unlawfully. It is commonplace that when you enter into a business contract; and/or need of service to be rendered, there is a "kola" (bribe) to be given, before it can be accomplished. So, now bribery, a form of corruption is wide spread even among the ordinary people of the city. And, astonishingly enough, even those from abroad who are concerned about the have-nots, are caught up on the way business is done.

The corruptions of the politicians make it impossible for workers to earn above minimum wage, or above the stagnant monthly salary. Average workers – either blue or white collar – are unhappy nowadays with their wages and salaries because it's not enough to cover the individual's purchasing power in the market. Therefore, many of the workers tend to borrow money and spend it before they receive their weekly or monthly salary. They are overextended before they get paid.

Public transportation is an eyesore. Many vehicles are just plain raggedy. Despite many of them being ordered off the streets, by the city officials, the owners and drivers refuse to remove them. If they take the vehicles off the street, that would be the end of their livelihood. But the sad reality is that they should be off the streets because a passenger can get injured. When either trying to get inside the vehicle - or about to sit down in the vehicle, or even when trying to depart from the vehicle, a passenger can get hurt or scraped. And, that's because the iron seats are worn and raggedy and have hardly any cushions on them. What's more, passengers have to watch out for the floors. The floors of many vehicles have holes in them. Passengers can easily be injured as they hurry inside, as they rush to get to their destination on time.

The consequence after living like this for a while is an, "I don't care" attitude emitted from many of the people. This contributes considerably to dirtiness of the streets and the rowdiness of the people – Paradise is a city in demise.

Goldteeth says, "Corruption is disseminating, all over the place."

# HUMAN ENVIRONMENT

# HUMAN ENVIRONMENT

## CONFRONTATION WITH THE LAWYER

I had made plans with Goldteeth to visit a friend on his go duty. But I also had suspicions about my lawyer that had begun to really bother me. So I took a detour to the Land Reacquisition Unit to verify that they had received the payment for the property on which I was to build.

I immediately discovered that not only had they not received any money; the so called Lawyer had given me a forged receipt. So clever was he that he even had the UBA (United Bank of Africa) checking account number on it. Where he slipped up, however, was in not having a Paradise City seal embossed on it. I was furious. I knew he was planning to get away with my money!

I left urgent messages for him to call me as soon as possible at a legitimate lawyer's number. I knew I had a fight on my hands to get my money back. But rather than dwell on this crisis, I kept my promise to go with Goldteeth to his friend's workplace.

## HOSPITAL ASPECT

Strolling along the neighborhoods in the city, Goldteeth continued to be excited. We had spotted a few hospitals. Having seen their untidy appearances, I could not hold my breath! I immediately asked him his point of view on how they are being managed by the administration.

"Well," he explains, "Our hospitals are not always managed properly, because the caring for the patients is not at its best." He elaborates on how the system works in many of the public hospitals in the city, and how patients are frequently jam-packed in the emergency rooms. "If a person has money, they would not bother to check into any of the public hospitals."

"Why, "I asked. "My friend," his face appeared sad, and instead of answering right away, he appears to be summoning up manly courage to continue. "At times the patients will be crying from pain. The nurse or doctor will just walk by." As he sadly spoke about how "The healthcare professionals act as if they have no heart towards the patients – even if they are screaming out, they pay little or no attention toward the crying patient! But if you are a well – known patient, well, it is then the nurse or doctor will pause for a moment and ask, what is the problem?"

There is no consistent pattern of care. The nurse or doctor may talk to the patient and promise to be back. This seems to just make the pain more aggravating- because it is a well-known fact that - only if you are lucky will the doctor ever return to a patient as promised. "I will be right back" is an often-used escape mechanism. Usually, the patient would be there just suffering for hours – before he or she receives the treatment he or she deserves. The time value has not been factored into the equation of patient care.

At times, Goldteeth ascertained that the patient who died is given no dignity either. The dead body is not cleaned or covered occasionally in a quiet room, but usually simply pushed into the public corridor - until an orderly comes to carry it to the morgue. Meanwhile, the bad odor of death permeates the area and a passerby may just vomit.

Some of these hospitals may not even have medication to dispense to patients who are lucky to even be treated by a doctor. Often treatment and medication are given largely because of a favor. In other words, a good turn must happen first – some sort of pay off.

Nevertheless, if the doctor assists a patient, with or without a payoff, the procedure is usually this: the doctor will advise the patient to go to the pharmacy to purchase the prescribed medication. The pharmacy owner happens to be related to the doctor, or be a friend of the doctor. As the patient follows the doctor's directive - and goes to the pharmacist to pick up medication, the patient usually finds that the price to be astronomical. There is usually a kick-back added on to the payment for the doctor. Thus, the medication becomes unaffordable and far out of reach for the patient. This ultimately leaves the patient with out medication and with an untreated ailment of disease.

I interjected, "Wait a minute, do you remember how hospitals used to be maintained before corruption was at its peak?" I reminded Goldteeth how the hospitals were maintained back in the day: "They were kept clean and the doctors and nurses were compassionate to everyone who needed treatment! They were always ready to treat patients and disperse medication - in a timely fashion and with accuracy – whether you had money or not." Individual was seen by doctors. Even if you did not have money to buy the medication prescribed, the doctors and nurses would dispense medications that were appropriated to the patients to help minimize the patient's pain, ailment or disease." Goldteeth was nodding his head in agreement – with everything I said.

"Apart from that, you rarely saw a dead body lie in the hospital corridor - without it being attended to immediately", I continued. "When a patient stepped into the hospital, the idea of who knew the patient was of slight significance. Yes, favoritism was there, but minimal. It was not as rampant as it is today. In previous times, patients were treated without preferential treatment."

My next thoughts focused on the overcrowded situation. I exclaimed, "So far, I am worried about the throng of patients in many of the emergency rooms. With so many people, how can they possibly be helped?" I asked my associate what could be the solution to the unprofessional management in the public hospitals by the administration. He has no immediate reply.

After a while, a solution ran through my mind. I spoke with Goldteeth about easing overcrowding. My idea was speckled with concern about whether it could be implemented succinctly, correctly and efficiently, without political maneuvering. My solution to hospital overcrowding is as follows: Have the Paradise City council create a separate Medical Office located nearby. A doctor and nurse practitioner could attend to the patients whose ailments do not warrant admission. They could be treated and then sent home. This would be an out-patient facility and could supplant the current situation where everyone, no matter what condition they are in is just packed in the one area together. Yes, a separate facility for the milder ailments would be a tremendous help.

It also made sense to me that even though there was a shortage of manpower, the few employees who work there should help each other. Caring for the individuals is a must and should come first. This type of mindset of helpfulness would stimulate productivity. There should be an execution of patient care procedures. This would be more efficient. Things would move quicker and ease the overcrowding.

"Furthermore," I expanded my idea, "the Paradise City Council should set aside a budget for the procurement of medication which should be monitored with strict accountability standards." I went on and on. I was on a roll! I came up with a structured plan to dispatch medications. "Finally, there should be a plan on how the medications are dispersed within the hospital", I told Goldteeth.

As we continued to roam along the public hospital's corridor, I observed that both the visitors and the patients, including myself, were sweating like a cold beer that had been sitting on ice – and then was placed in a hot room for 5 minutes – shedding water all over the place.

So, the generators go off intermittently, for the benefit of a sweetheart deal being made. Whatever the powers-that-be are doing - in this hospital, without the air-conditioning, the people are burning up this building. When the lights go out everyone – the patients, the healthcare professionals, the visitors – absolutely everyone in this hospital are in danger. They are in complete darkness unless; they have a generator as a back up until the electricity comes on again.

The only alternative to this scenario is to use candles, or lantern with kerosene – if you are not rich. But, cheap kerosene emits carbon monoxide and a thick, black smoke. And of course, the smoke is going to create a new health hazard. Everyone will be inhaling the fumes and this will cause a more serious breathing problem particularly for those individuals who already have a respiratory disease, such as asthmatics.

This was not the case before, I thought to myself. At that time, NAPA – an electrical company - made sure that the electricity was turned on all the time. No one had excessive influence – especially the power to turn the electrical current off and on. This mismanagement of the electricity is causing people to get sick - and making the patients even sicker. Workers, doctors, the housekeeper, everyone who came to work there, could suffocate in this environment, especially if he or she is not getting to breathe some fresh air. And the extremely hot, enclosed buildings of the public hospitals have none.

"Look", he exclaimed. Goldteeth passionately wanted to show me something. "Many of the equipments for the hospitals are out-dated."

"Why?" I questioned. He continued in his vernacular, "The hospitals administration does not have money to buy sophisticated equipment that would last longer and are more durable. Instead, a second-hand one is purchased, so the equipment has no specific life span. In other words, this equipment can easily break down, which leads to repairing them over and over again."

Note having dilapidated equipment is not due to the hospitals having no money, as is always proclaimed. It is just that there is no honest accountability on how money is appropriated and is being managed. The money is horribly mismanaged. For instance, when equipment is malfunctioning constantly, the administration sends in the estimate to the procurement department to buy a new one. The estimate is always inflated and includes a personal kick-back. Next, the equipment arrives -. Though it looks shiny and new, it is not brand new. It is refurbished. It is second-hand. It is repainted, re-polished, and renovated. The purpose of doing business with these specific manufacturers is not for the betterment of the hospital, but for embezzlement. Part of the appropriated money is pilfered. This is constant and consistent.

What is worse, there is no watch-dog committee; no one to question why used equipment is being purchased instead of new equipment. Thus, the very people that the hospital should serve, the patients, end up staying in the hospital longer than the usual time frame or their disorder or individual treatment because of the constant equipment malfunctions!

I said to Goldteeth, "You know, before corruption become rampant, the hospital administration used money to buy new equipment – old, used equipment was not even thought of." We agreed how, above all, the hospital officials would scrutinize the warranty of the durability, effectiveness and the life span of newly purchased equipment. "The hospital officials had to give an account of how money was spent." I pronounced, "It is a shame that corruption is cherished daily."

In the end, after looking at this hospital environment, we should be mindful that the value of human lives should never be judged by their political connections. A patient should not be looked upon by how rich he or she is. Caring for the patient, after all, is an essential which requires the governing body's richest resources and excellence in fulfillment. Sadly, in the present circumstance, if a person does not have money - it seems so hopeless to the people who then begin to rationalize as follows: "if I am sick, why should I bother to check into the public hospital. I will be treated with neglect and without dignity."

# HUMAN ENVIRONMENT

## DUG-HOLE WELL

"I am thirsty. I feel like drinking water", I whispered. Goldteeth laughed. Then I asked him why he laughed. He replies that, "The water which the hustlers are selling is 'clean water', which I think is not clean at all! However some are truly clean, but it depends on who the supplier is."

What a catch-22! Can you imagine, I am thirsty and I don't know whom to trust to provide me with a cool drink of water? Many unreliable suppliers just take their water from a dug-hole well, which is unhygienic. They pour it into a transparent bag. They seal the bag and then sell the so-called 'clean water' on the street. If you are an unsuspecting buyer, you could get very sick. It is left to the buyer to know which brand name uses hygienic manufacturing practices, and which brand does not. If you as - the buyer cannot distinguish between the brands, then you will likely catch cholera by frequently drinking the impure water.

Besides the infection of cholera from the water, many of the areas are unsanitary where the dug-holes exist. For example, I spotted a couple of locations for the dug-hole wells - where the dumping area is practically adjacent. And that type of area is always saturated with flies. Imagine! The water is siphoned from wells that are full of flies. The flies are polluting the water. This is the water that is going to the households.

The idea of the dug-hole wells came into existence when the government neglected to repair the water reservoirs. As a result they dried up. And so the tap water pipes in the homes became useless, and there is no water in them. The dug-holed wells are here for necessity. They became the city's only means of obtaining water.

However, I remembered - the city used to be full of tap water – that was of good use. The water was clean and drinkable. The reservoir had a water purification system. At the moment, there is no such reservoir. And the government does not seem to care to rebuild them.

# HUMAN ENVIRONMENT

## THE POOR ARE NOT CLOSE TO THE RICH

"Another thing I notice," Goldteeth said with much alarm, "there are no bridges between the rich and the poor." There are so many examples of this and the repercussions that ensue. Just take for example the medical conditions and the high unemployment issue.

The lack of efficient medical treatment for poor people turns into a scenario whereby people become physically and mentally weak and sick people cannot look for a job. Despite unemployment being so high, the people are so downtrodden that they do not even look for something to do in their daily lives. They don't have the energy. They are idle.

So many people look like they are fasting. When you think of fasting you think of fasting for a purpose. These people are just hungry and they have become paupers.

"What can be done about this?" I asked as I interrogated Goldteeth.

"Well," he responded, "nothing can be done to improve the lives of paupers because the leaders and the rich are always conniving.

It was obvious that Goldteeth was right. The politicians do not drive around to observe the conditions of the poor in these poverty stricken neighborhoods. As a result of neglect, the poor constantly collapsed, are succumbing to extreme hunger and thirst. They pass out or pass on, right there on the road sides. Were it not for realizing that corruption existed, it would appear that the politicians could not possibly be aware of the paupers on the streets, and the milieu or death that exists there.

I remembered back again, in the old days, poverty may not have been completely non-existent, but it was in moderation. The economy was stimulated. The people, who wanted to work - got a job and enjoyed their hard earned wages. They bought food and other household items; the necessary things to maintain their lives. Then those who were able to feed themselves developed high self-esteem. Consequently, they could think constructively and be creative. People then in general, were stand up hard-working people.

Today, by contrast, people have pervasive low self-esteem. Many people are not working and – therefore, are dirt poor. This leads to hostility and meanness. You can see the mean look on their faces as you pass people on the streets, as we go about our daily journey.

# HUMAN ENVIRONMENT

## EATING IN UNSANITARY PLACES

Before continuing the next morning on our brigade, we decided first to eat. We stopped in a nearby restaurant. It is not attractive, particularly to those who come from overseas. I tell Goldteeth that I don't want to stay. He tells me wait. I tell him it is very untidy and I am very uncomfortable. He says to me, "Stay, I know what you are seeing." "It is unclean in here," I am adamant. He says customers who prefer not to eat here just get their food and go home with it. I said, "The dust from the road is coming in and getting all over prepared food. I don't want to eat here, nor do I want to take it home." What is fascinating is that people who are here eating just eat as if nothing is wrong. I stand up. We leave.

Let's go in here, says Goldteeth, as we had walked a few paces down the road, silently. I was brooding. I was almost not hungry anymore. I looked at the next restaurant suspiciously. It was enclosed with fans. I heard music playing. I felt relieved. We went in. Although the tables and chairs were too close to each other, I told myself to mind my temper and we sat down. I ordered a simple traditional breakfast of guinea pea porridge with some cakes, a fried bread of ground black-eyed peas and Goldteeth had the farina with cassava bread which consists of ground cassava and baking soda mix. We both ordered coffee. Then I said to Goldteeth, "Let's have sardines!" Goldteeth laughed ridiculously, "Yes, yes, let's have sardines." I thought to myself, "only the rich order sardines on a regular basis. This must be quite a treat for Goldteeth."

When our food came, someone bumped my table. I had to grab my plate to keep my food from sliding off the table. I felt so embarrassed and wanted to tell the other person to watch it. I remembered to be quiet as I noticed everyone seemed to have their plates encircled with a forearm and hand, as if to keep the very same from happening to them. "Oh my God, we eat like…" I shut up and finished my sentence in my mind … uncivilized people, protecting our food as if an animal was on the prowl, to snatch it from us.

Goldteeth must have read my mind and said the eaters must use the hand that is free to prevent their food from being knocked down. I wanted some more coffee. I looked up for our waitress. I can't find her and everyone is so bundled up together. Then I realized they don't wear uniforms. So how was I to know who was to serve me, with the crowd of people sitting, eating and having lazy talks along with those standing up talking and relating? After Goldteeth found the waitress, we had two more cups of coffee and a good lazy talk after eating. Then we decided to take a bird's eye view of the Paradise City.

Goldteeth and I took a stroll. It was a nice, cool morning. We are proceeding slowly, but steadily. I tap on my partner's shoulder to call his attention to an unsanitary market. As we step into the market, my escort observes a seller cooking her lunch by the gutter full of flies. There was an unpleasant odor. We pause -. I can't control my curiosity. I am wondering how a human being could be in such an unhygienic surrounding? It gets worse.

Soon the trader finishes her cooking. Now she hurries and covers the food, and takes it to a more hygienic area. A safe place where there are no flies, so that she and her children can eat. She is going to a paved road nearby, not an unpaved one where you inhale the dust in your lungs. This is what I imagined. But, the rude awakening was that she sat right down with her children in the same dirty spot that she had cooked and began to eat their meal. Both of us watched in amazement.

We kept watching. As we were watching, one child was about to put the food into his mouth when a heap of flies swarmed over to him. And here they landed, on top of the food in his hand. The child does not worry to drive or shoo the flies away with his hands. It does seem that a few flies may have escaped before he put the food in his mouth, as we watched him eat and swallow. I, then, formed the opinion that the child must be really hungry at this time.

What are even more appalling than that is that a few yards away, we see a couple of teen boys urinating on the side where people are cooking and eating. I then postulate that the marketers do not care for their own health and well-being. I presume that others in the marketplace - do the same, eat and cook in a dirty, nasty, dusty, fly-ridden environment.

As we proceed, we hear a noise and look around to see where it came from. The dumping sound erupts like a river flowing from a hill and running into a valley – it sounds lovely. But, it is not that way at all. In fact, it is the combination of noise and filth that has captured our attention. There is a lady dumping garbage mixed with water into the dirty muddy gutter. There is certainly nothing lovely or nice about it!

I hadn't finished expressing my view about the whole scenario to my escort before he and I see a marketer laying her child down on a mat. The child's eyes are yellow. This suggests that her child is suffering from malaria fever. A mat is spread on a table and half of the child is covered with a scarf.

I am about to approach the mother to advise her to take the boy to a nearby hospital for treatment, before his sickness takes a toll on him. But I know I cannot show my hospitality openly. Otherwise, the mother who does know me would view my compassion as an insult. And, as I remembered, in this culture, she wouldn't heed my advice anyway.

My escort interrupted me, and began talking about the Paradise City Council and how they used to have the Sanitation Inspectors working.

How they were dispatched all over the various market places. The Sanitation Inspectors issued tickets to scofflaws. There were regulations that had to be abided by. No seller could sell in an obnoxious surround; the seller must sweep and wash down the area and the gutter; and they could not have any food matter in an area bombarded with flies. Whoever violated the rules of Hygiene was issued a ticket. They had to pay a fine. They had to clean it up to continue to stay in business. These were the rules.

Then, at least, most of the marketer's areas were clean and conducive to eat in. They could even rest there (for a nap). The sellers even had helpers who would stand watch over their goods - and keep their businesses going as they rested. Today, no one sees a Sanitation Inspector around. No one is going from one market place to another - inspecting anything. "No one is checking for unsanitary market spots -", my escort declared.

Although - many of the hygienic hospitals of the past were not perfect and could have been improved, it was never as bad as what I see today. Consequently, my concern about the unsanitary conditions is so overwhelming. Diseases - such as malaria fever and cholera can affect the entire market place. This area could be very contagious; not only to the marketers, but the buyers, the little innocent children and all that come into contact here. I felt frightened for everyone. I was down and my thoughts were very sad.

# HUMAN ENVIRONMENT

## GANGSTERS' ROLE DURING ELECTION TIME

As the election is approaching, Goldteeth and I are envisioning the outcome. Will the election results be fair and peaceful: without rigging and violence? Will there be gangsters involved? Our questions would soon be answered.

We continue promenading the streets. It's filled with different political factions. We see and hear various different party supporters and their opinions. As we pause at an interval, one Party gave us a synopsis of their ideology; what they stand for, and how they would improve the city.

Suddenly gun shots erupted. As we look around, very far off -, we see people starting to run for their lives. As people are stampeding in our direction, we can see several are bruised with blood splattered on their clothes. The police suddenly appeared and bombarded the area with tear gas. It floods the area to the extent that my partner and I have to 'take to our heels' to keep from inhaling it. Although we are not close to the hooligans and the point of the chaos, the smoke from the tear gas is thick and closing in.

This commotion, the running and the unnecessary bloodshed did not quench the rioters' thirst for mass confusion. Instead, it escalated and the mass hysteria spread to another neighborhood where different gangsters gathered. They support the banners of the politicians. The gangsters start beating people, while other onlookers are knifed and drop on the spot.

What is strange is that we don't see even one single political candidate out there campaigning. The party's that are running are supposed to be manned by legitimate campaign staff – not gangsters.

"What is going on? Why are gangsters allowed to take over the campaign?" I asked Goldteeth. Goldteeth explained that the gangsters are on the street to intimidate the voters and to subdue them. Their goal is to silence the people and stop them from voting for their favorite candidate. The political candidates are the ones who are paying the gangsters to keep the confusion. They give the gangsters a lump sum of money to operate in this barbaric manner during the time of the election.

So, the gangsters go where the opposing political party is campaigning and start a riot. I have my answer. I no longer have to query. But Goldteeth has more, "In addition, gangsters are like cults who grow in number -. They take the law into their own hands: they create riots and kill citizens who do not bend to their orders." He explains that craziness to me is that - if a politician is weak and has few supporters but wants to win the election by all means necessary, this is what they do – spread fear. Thus, I see, the cults are part and parcel of politics so to speak -. They have become part of the system - while the citizens are paying in blood for it. Therefore, the political system is corroded with corruption and violence. "It is more of a criminal enterprise - than a system of government." states Goldteeth.

On the contrary, in the early days, some politicians used to have individual rascals whom the candidates paid in return for protection against other political rivals. They were hired, more in turn, as body guards. Then those sentinels recommended themselves to protect the candidates during the campaign, because they believed in the candidate. None of those scoundrels formed a cult-type group. Today, they are a faction of wild intolerance, as they go as far as they could to interrupt the opponent's supporters. Today, they are not only hired for protection but they also purposely create disturbances.

Violence and killing was not a substantial part of the old scheme. In those days, any political party that won the election would stage a thank you party for the important supports. The rigging of an election was not a rampant practice -. It was minimal. What was done unethically back then was done behind closed doors –, not done openly. Hence, many politicians were not as shameful in the public eye.

I looked at my friend Goldteeth and exclaimed, "Today's politician does not govern. They do not seem to work for the people - at all. But they campaign vigorously, in person or with representatives. And some blatantly hire thugs as their representatives!"

Goldteeth said, "Irepo, You got it. They do not govern, they only campaign."

# HUMAN ENVIRONMENT

## URINATING ON THE STREET

My eyes landed on a woman stooping in the bushes. "Watch, what is the woman stooping down doing?" I inquired with much awe.

My escort followed my gaze. He looked in the direction of the woman stooping at the side of the road, next to the grass, in an open area and laughed. "She is urinating and is not ashamed because she has to let out the urine urgently."

What happens if the police see her?" I asked.

He says, "A policeman will not arrest her if she rips open a couple of Nira (money)." Hence, I realized bribery allows the scofflaws to get away with it – they won't be arrested.

From what I could see, pride is out of the window amongst the people of Paradise City. And - bribery is a way of life – as it is even at times offered openly and accepted openly.

"What happened to the public latrines which used to be around the city in the old days?" I interrogated.

# HUMAN ENVIRONMENT

## OFFICE MESSENGER ENVIRONMENT ON THE STREET AND AT WORK

As we continue walking and observing the dirty scenery, that catches our eyes, I hear a loud bell ringing. I turn to see it attached to a bicycle. The continuous loud ringing comes closer and forces me to jump the edge of the sidewalk. I pull my partner quickly to the side as well. Seeing my panic he tells me not to be nervous. It is just the messengers riding fast and alarming the pedestrians to move to the side - so the bicycles may not hurt them or hit them.

When he mentioned the word messenger, it reminded me of how they used to behave in the offices. They used to take folders and files that were ready for delivery off the shelves. Basically, these messengers' -, particularly the civil service ones' -, major duties were to transfer the folders (be it classified or unclassified), from one section to another section of the department. There was a unique way that they would handle security of the folders also. If an unknown person, or an ex-employee came in and asked for a document from the folder, and even if they needed it urgently – which likely would mean by-passing official permission from the head of the department, the officer in charge, the messenger who sat by the entrance door - would discourage the person who requested the document by telling him or her that the folder is no longer in the department. Even upon insistence by the would-be procurer, the messenger on the door would go further to state that all the folders have been relocated to the archives, and it takes time to retrieve them. It cannot be done quickly. My partner nodded his head in confirmation.

Then out of frustration the person who wanted the document would tip the messenger, a sure fire way of getting the document and with the expectation that a change to the rules would be made in his favor. Of course, now the messenger takes the money secretly, and has a change of thought, and says, "Oh, I just remembered, your folder is among the others that we left in the drawer for revision. Come inside." That is the messenger's way of confirming that the document will now be given to the person. Of course, the whole time this is going on, the boss is "unaware" of this scheme. What a scenario! And now today, instead of this just happening here and there, this is an on-going situation. So, instead of things getting better in time, as the natural way life should go, it has become much worse. The system has not changed for the better. Bribery has not been eradicated. Where it was once rare, it is now an everyday occurrence.

"It is horrendous for any messenger to indirectly solicit a bribe", I pronounced to my partner. Again and again when people see that corruption is not curtailed by the politicians, corruption then spreads like a virus. Even the low-income, low-level workers and citizens pick it up, as a way of life; it's a way of making a few extra Niras.

# HUMAN ENVIRONMENT

## CULTURAL ACTIVITIES

With our tireless energy, we are still wondering whether to catch public transportation or continue walking on this hot, sunny day. After a while, I hear the beating of drums and ask my partner to explain the purpose of the drumming.

Then Goldteeth said to me, "Let us walk toward the beating location. That way, you can see for yourself." I concurred with him. We both hastened to see what the beating of the drums was all about.

We reached the area; Goldteeth narrated the cultural aspect of the gathering. It was a festival with a group of performing masqueraders. They have a three tiered ritual comprised of dancing, drumming, and dispersing. After that, they initially gather in one area and then spread out to perform throughout the city for the amusement of the people. This type of amusement with the 3 tiers was different from the one I remembered from back in my day.

Prior to these current amusements, there was a different type of masquerade gathering at the Square, usually in the center of the city. At the center of the square would be a leader, the OYAA. The OYAA would be there to greet, direct and control the masquerade. He would also, as the leader, authorize the killing of a goat as a sacrifice to the spirits. When the ritual is successfully completed, there again would be an eruption of the beating of the drums. Some masqueraders would dance; while others would start flogging one another with a flexible stick. All the masqueraders carried a stick, a symbol of strength that earned them respect. The traditional festival always lasted for seven days. But, then things began to change. Nowadays, after the first day, or any other day thereafter, they stopped appearing. You may or may not see this particular amusement play out its seven day stint. The usual amusements have become sporadic. Then this traditional style, OYAA style, with the killing of the goat has ended, and is no longer practiced.

On another occasion, earlier that morning, we witnessed a different group of paradisers, the AAYO Festival. Each group has their own leader. They start at different points in the day; all the groups would converge at Iduma, a neighborhood in the city. There, the most respected leader, called - the ADMU, would be there for all to see. All of the AAYO groups pay him respect. Then the drumming would begin again, as the individual groups fell into the procession. At last they would scatter all around the city again, and the ritual would end as it had begun, with the groups each performing dancing activities - for the various neighborhoods.

All who participate in the AAYO Festival are in uniforms that are professionally designed and seamed. Every AAYO participant (no women) has a white transparent cloth that covers his face. Their attire is long and drags on the floor behind them like a train. Each AAYO also carries a club which is made from the coconut tree branches. The club is used to touch the onlookers as a sign of admiration. However, if they sighted a friend, who in reality they harbor resentment towards - or who is considered truly a foe; or, if it is someone they just don't like, some would lash out and beat that unfortunate onlooker. What's more, they had the power to get away with it. There is nothing - a person who is being a victim can do - except to run away to avoid being beaten. The impunity is like an unwritten law. No one says or does anything.

At the AAYO's discretion, he may deign to lift his veil to reveal who he is. If he does not choose to do so, he just does not and his identity stays a secret and he just continues on with the rest of the procession.

Other AAYOS use the club to touch onlookers as they recite an incantation. When they finish the onlookers may give the AAYO a gift, such as money, to show admiration. In this way, many of the AAYOS end up rich at the evening's end. A festival can be quite profitable for an AAYO. Not bad for a day long festival.

On another day, a bright cool, sunny day, my pilot and I are walking along a BASIN area, and I spot a large group there. Curiously I asked, "What are they doing over yonder?"

My partner informs me that today will be Rigatta Boat Racing Contest. We reach the location where I could see how it is being arranged. Since my partner is well informed and very familiar with the boat racing, I gave him the honor of explaining it to me - instead of asking someone else to give me the background of Rigatta contest.

According to him, a community leader organized it. All of the racing boats are decorated. Music is supplied to entertain the audience. When the race is about to commence, the racing boats are lined up in a straight line with the referee making sure that the lineup is even. When everything is under control, the referee blows the whistle and all of the boats take off with high speed.

Each boat has to reach a certain designated area where another referee is waiting. That referee is stationed at that point to make sure that every-one of the racers reaches the point before turning and going back to the beginning. The first boat to get back is declared the winner for that set. The procedure goes on for a day and ends before dusk.

This kind of wonderful cultural activity is less in existence now - due to the political corruption that is rampant in the city. Thus, many amusements and cultural activities are rare nowadays. Occasionally, though, one or two may surface -. The citizens are not as enthusiastic to participate in - or watch them as they once had been. Cultural activities are not highly valued or recognized as they once were.

# HUMAN ENVIRONMENT

## MILDEW ON HOUSES

"So far there are not too many attractive houses to catch my eyes fancy," I remarked. Since my guide and I have been promenading around the city that day, I have noticed so many of the houses had dirty appearances.

My partner replied that, "Painting of the houses to show off attraction is not a wise thing to do."

"Why?" I asked.

He explained, "Keeping up the appearance of your house would be a sign of prosperity and would make you an instant target for robbery, because it is almost impossible to maintain a beautiful façade on the exteriors of the houses. A majority of the roads are dusty and, besides - the heat, the glue on the painted houses attracts the dust. This has disfigured their appearance." Goldteeth talked at length about the filth and the disgrace of the houses. He spoke of how the houses are all full of mildew and mold. This, of course, will spoil the houses' attractiveness.

The dismal appearance of the homes, the mildew on the exterior, and the fear being of robbed all cause despair, ambiguity, and apathy among the homeowners. So they just do not care anymore. They have lost pride in the upkeep of their homes. Even many of the officials of the Paradise City Council and State have houses that lack regular painting. This is just how many of the houses look. This is just how people live. People who once lived a better life have been reduced to this.

We move on to a well renowned location called, "LOCK-BEACH". Speaking of unattractive buildings, I was in shock as we passed through this area. Many of these buildings - that were once so beautiful, as well as the State Buildings, have also lost their attractiveness. They, too, are full of mold and mildew! The gutters are full of stagnant dirty water. In addition, the lagoon water which used to be blue in color has even turned into a brackish dirty yellow muck. This is such a sad thing to see.

I notice that the beautiful, elegant, pine trees which used to serve as shades for the LOCK-BEACH goers and homes are hemmed up, one on top of the other, making the area very unattractive. "Since you have traveled to the United States a lot of changes have occurred" remarked my escort. He told me the money appropriated for cleaning and revamping the city was diverted to do something else. Yet, there was something else…, which sounded more like a priority for the politicians.

Consequently, the place has just gone downhill. One thing is clear, and that is, "Paradise was cleaner in the old days, much cleaner than what you and I have seen so far, right?" I said, shaking my head and questioning my partner at the same time. I went into a monologue, almost a diatribe, as if I were talking to myself. I was upset and angry. The gutters for the buildings used to be cleaned and washed thoroughly to prevent dirtiness and smelling and odor. That is not done any longer. But what is being seen frequently instead are just all of these smelling areas around the city. The cleaning that is in place is just occasional, and it is not thoroughly done. My associate told me that - the citizens believe that the cleaning is just a lip service -. As soon as the cleaners are gone -, the surroundings heaped up with more and more garbage. This is a joke, I thought to myself.

# HUMAN ENVIRONMENT

## CORRUPTION IN EXCESSIVE PRACTICE

"Corruption cannot be condoned! And it should not be a part of economic development!" Goldteeth affirmed. "Corruption drags community development back into a rudimentary economic development and motivates citizens to follow suit. It influences citizens not to be compassionate towards their fellow citizens – especially when it comes to economic survival.

Corruption widens the gap between the rich and the poor. And when it is not minimized it makes the poor even poorer. You can see the very examples of this, with the paupers, as they are desperate and begging to meet and to come in contact with the self-sufficient. They are hoping that they may be hired by the affluent as servants. They are begging for their daily bread, to be noticed and to be employed.

As bad as corruption may be for a town, city or nation, and its indigenous people, excessive corruption is always the enemy to tourism. As a result, tourism is minimal to nonexistent. Moreover, corruption can make a nation that is developing - rewind – and go totally backwards. The quality of life that was once known is upset and overturned. The people become apathetic and corrupt. On top of this, the people and their offspring become apathetic and corrupt. On top of this, the people and their offspring become more and more ignorant to the right way of life. And because the politicians ignore the criticism of corruption from their own people - and the rest of the civilized countries, it just proliferates.

"Excessive corruption contributes to illness. And even death!" stated Goldteeth. He continued, "Corruption has reduced the citizen's longevity; especially, the poor and those who constantly are seeking their daily bread morning, afternoon, and again in the evening. Because there is little - or no

- help from their fellow man, these very same people's life and health are in jeopardy. You can see when you look around, how frayed and fragile they look as they walk around begging and searching for good Samaritans.

As Goldteeth winded up, he said, "The have-nots constantly move from place to place, wherever there is a party or a ceremonial activity they go; hoping that they may be given leftover food to eat for that day".

# HUMAN ENVIRONMENT

## DRIVING CONFUSION

As Goldteeth and I set out on foot on a bright, summer morning somewhere around 9:30 a.m., I cautioned him to watch out for the reckless drivers as we proceeded walking from one street to another. Before I finished giving pieces of advice to my associate, I heard the screeching car brakes, echoed with a woman cursing and screaming. The woman had a baby on her back. I panicked when I heard the loud noise and began focusing on the commotion. But my partner quickly calmed me to act normal. So we both stood there and stared at the commotion.

The woman staggered and leaned on the car, which was on the sidewalk. The driver got out - and looked at her. I'm thinking to myself, how in the world did he get on the sidewalk? We are watching the driver and woman, to see how the two would resolve their predicament. Then, the woman stood straight up. It appears that neither she nor the baby was injured. But there is no doctor around to examine them either. All of a sudden the driver jumped into his car and kicked on off from the scene. And the woman, without any further abusive words also moved on as if nothing happened to her. And so, we continue.

As we scramble from street to street – to avoid of being hit by cars driven by these outrageous drivers, we see a heavy collision. One car was hit from behind – a tailgate. Both drivers got out of their respective cars and began to fight. Neither examined their car. Neither thought to look to see how serious the damage was. Traffic began to back up as these two were going at it. Drivers who had no patience to wait until traffic flow was restored to normal drove into the side walk to bypass the heavy traffic congestion. The collided drivers could not move their cars to the side. They try, in vain, to push their cars to the side of the road. It becomes too cumbersome for them by themselves, so to make money hustlers offer help to move the cars. Slowly and gradually, the traffic returns to normal.

But what is normal? While this calamity is going on, petty traders and hustlers are crossing streets and stopping traffic to try to sell their goods to pedestrians, drivers, and absolutely anyone. They are helping to disturb the flow of traffic. The hustlers are pushing their goods with no concern for whether the cars are going to hit them. As this goes on, cars are cutting in and out of traffic haphazardly. They are knowingly blocking the intersection between cars and buses, as if trying to see where they want to go. What a dismal transportation system, with major traffic congestion. To top it all off, it is preventing the pedestrians from crossing safely.

Meanwhile, we are roaming the streets hoping to find a safe area where the traffic congestion would be abated. Somewhere, the pedestrians, as well as the cars, buses, wheel-barrow and motor cycle riders would move freely. Less than fifteen minutes later, as we are both searching for this utopia, wishing for a place where traffic would be minimized, we reach an open area with round-about driving, where the traffic congestion is reduced.

At this area, we spotted several cars, buses -. They were all standing still, frozen. It was almost as if traffic officers had stopped vehicles at a check point. On the contrary, each vehicle, in trying to beat the traffic congestion, came to a stalemate. The configuration of vehicles looked like a one giant cross formation on the street.

The traffic is terrible. There is no alternative to this fight since there are no functioning police. They are there, but they're not effective. That is, they are not enforcing any of the traffic regulations and laws, because they can do nothing to divert traffic to an alternate route. The police are not outnumbered and overwhelmed with rough drivers. The rude, crude behavior of the wheel-barrow pushers and the mass frenzy of boisterous, road rage is the mind-set that has taken over.

On top of this, the police are out in the burning sun, with little fresh air. The roads are rotten. The air is thick with a sickening, noxious order made worse by the heat. The only alternative in this configuration is that the drivers outside the traffic jam begin to drive onto the sidewalk, to get out of there. Even though this alarming process endangers the people on the sidewalk – the drivers don't care. So now the poor pedestrians must take to their heels - in order to not allow the agitated drivers to or even kill them.

Goldteeth tapped me on the shoulder, and explained that the traffic congestion would not be eradicated or minimized as long as the traffic officers are not happy with their monthly salaries. Ah ha! There is always more to the story. In other words, a decent salary would go a long way. Thus, the salary is an issue. So if it were a good salary, it would stimulate them to work more efficiently in curbing dangerous drivers on the streets. Almost sounds like a bribe, except for the fact I know the extenuating circumstances that the police are under. What a problem this is.

While he was explaining the predicament, a couple of vehicles drove up on the sidewalk near us. They had to drive about one hundred feet before they could get back on the streets. What's crazier is, as soon as one driver started to drive on the sidewalk, another one followed suit – and another – and another! What we observed was horrendous, pitiful and scary. Due to the zigzag of uncontrollable drivers, we give up, exited this place and went further up, over, down and around to another safer road.

# HUMAN ENVIRONMENT

## DIRECT AND INDIRECT STEALING

Direct stealing can be defined as when a person deliberately takes someone else's belongings, without permission. In other words, he takes something that is attractive to him or of value. It's a little harder to do because it is easier to get caught. So, direct stealing in one way seems to be under control because thieves have a fear of being caught, and the consequences are great. You can be beaten and/or put in jail. I asked my guide to give me his view on this.

"Concerning direct stealing, too many people are guilty of this today and there is no evidence that it will be wiped out soon", Goldteeth stated. "So many people steal, or attempt to steal. When they get caught, they are severely beaten - if there are no police around to arrest them. The reason for the severe beating is to let others know stealing is bad, and not to influence unemployed poor people, who just don't have money to take care of their family to participate.... How can you steal from someone who already has nothing? When people see a person caught for stealing someone else's property, they will learn a lesson too. So any person caught - could be killed without any mercy."

As my accomplice and I promenade along the street, I hear a loud noise. As we continue to walk, the noise becomes a little less muffled. It's a voice calling for help. And we hear the call over and over, in a monotonous manner. We follow the sound and see two guys being beaten with different kinds of sticks by a crowd. We both rush to see if we could rescue them. To our surprise, the beating is very severe. The crowd yelled at us to keep our distance. So we both halt and begin backing off. The police arrive and all the people suddenly vanish like lightening. We also move away through fear of being called upon as witnesses. I realize these are possibly thieves that have stolen something. On top of this, I notice the crowd is in fear, the thieves are in fear, and the passerby just walking up is in fear too. But he then states that the person who engages in the direct stealing usually prevails. It seems – nowadays – that the person who is doing an evil act has the power.

Indirect stealing is much more common. Goldteeth starts to explain to me how indirect stealing comes into being. For instance, it could begin in a family…

"When two brothers are not equally blessed or talented or have the same amount of money; or when one is favored more by the father, the one who is slighted will fell hurt, envy and hatred. He may even try to make voodoo on his own sibling - by maybe asking that the father not favor, or leave property to him or not pay attention to the rich or more talented sibling. Corruption often breaks up families and opens the door to evil.

# HUMAN ENVIRONMENT

## CRITIQUE OF NEWSPAPERS ON CORRUPTION

The more I contemplated the facts, the more concerned I became about why it was that the majority of the populace did not seem too disapproved of this corrupt way of living -. It just gets worse and worse. And they say to do nothing! So, I quietly asked Goldteeth, "Why do you think corruption disseminates through Paradise City like a venereal disease"?

"Well", Goldteeth began to explain -. He looked puzzled, and fell quiet too. "You know, this has been going on so long. People just don't talk about it anymore." He looked puzzled again. Was he saying the stealing by the Paradise city government of money and properties is so blatant, so meshed into society, that it's just not the talk of the town anymore? But then he said, "But there is more to it, than just that…"

My associated tried to explain this intricate web of craziness. "If a person becomes outspoken, it could be a life-threatening thing! Even murmuring about the condition to the wrong person can become a scary thing. People can get hurt - if it gets back to the wrong people that you are talking about their actions. If someone is making a lot of money off corruption and they are violent, they may hurt you or kill you for being a whistle-blower."

Goldteeth further explained, "Pilfering, stealing, embezzling, cutting corners, payoffs or other types of corruption are now tolls for doing business – not only by council members, and politicians, and government officials or even the petty crook, but also by the everyday layman. So a person cannot, and will not, dare advise his spouse to desist from accepting or being accommodating to a bribe from whomever they are seeking a contract, or help from. Today whether a person is rich or poor, the person must offer a 'KOLA'! Otherwise, the person will not be offered the contract - or be given any type of helping hand", he concluded.

Many newspapers such as, *The African Abroad, Daily times, Tribune, Daily Telegraph, Vanguard, Guardian, Punch* and *The Sun* occasionally eye the practice of corruption. But believe me; each one of the papers has a cunning way of critiquing corruption, because they fear that atrocities may befall their writers from the powers-that-be. So, they curb constantly commenting on corrupted individual politicians, the council and the government officials. But the writers believe in the freedom of speech. So they refuse to **desist**. But, there are only a few newspapers that focus on investigating and commenting on corruption.

Goldteeth picked up a few copies of the Nigerian newspapers and he spotted an article on corruption in *The Vanguard*. He read the story: *"A Case against Corruption"* by Abele Crapo. One quote was, "I honestly don't get it. If the Economic and Finance Crime commission (EFCC) is serious about arresting this hydra-headed monster called corruption, then they are going about it the wrong way."

I quickly intercepted Goldteeth to explain what he deduced from those words - before he reads any further. He explains in his own words that the EFCC doesn't bother to investigate the corrupted officials or even try to put a stop to the corruption instantly. He puts it bluntly, "However, if the EFCC really wanted to do so, before it got so out of hand, they would have done so long before it spread to the populace. They should not have let this happen."

*The Guardian* newspaper exposes and questions Federal Airport Authority of Nigeria (FAAN) about the government security agents. The question posted is based on the latest scandal story: INEC's Direct Data Capturing (DDC) machines were rumored to be stolen by the government security agents. There is a related story about an exposé on FAAN officials so that they do not go free without accounting for the whereabouts of the stolen machines.

In praise of the vigilantes of these papers, *the Punch* as well as *the Sun* paper talks about pilfering of DDC machines due to the unconcern and 'I don't care' attitude of the officials. *The Punch* revealed that the DDC machines disappeared at the Muritala Mohammed International Airport.

*The Sun* writers Willyeya and Olusola Balogun quoted Chief Olu Falae, "...the disappearance of the DDC machines was a sign that some people were already preparing to rig the forthcoming election... the election would not be free and fair."

Goldteeth finally inserted a point that corruption is the most warriors for the rigging of elections. It has becomes a custom for the majority of politicians to constantly do this, as the opportunity is in their hands. Therefore, only a few politicians are caught when practicing corruption; while most go free. Consequently, no one knows for sure how and when the 'hydra-headed monster' of corruption would be abated or eradicated.

# ECONOMIC ENVIRONMENT

# ECONOMIC ENVIRONMENT

## LABOR SURPLUS

I had some documents that needed typing, so I decided to get out and find a secretary. I wanted to write down everything the lawyer said to me as well as my findings on the state of things in Paradise City.

Accordingly, that particular morning, I decided to visit an Employment Office that was advertising. I took Goldteeth with me. When we got there, we were both surprised to see such a huge congregation of job-seekers, many of whom dressed neatly to impress their prospective employer. On the other hand, there were also quite a few who were not properly dressed. Out of curiosity, my Pilot and I managed to find our way past the crowd, into the office to find out, 'how many positions were available?'

Based on our observation, and without asking the employer the total number of applicants, we guessed that there were upwards of two hundred or more. The applicants looked so eager – too eager. You could see it in their faces and their posture. They were sitting on the edge of their seats. They look at each other and every applicant who walks through the door. They are showing signs that they are anxious to accept whatever wage rate the employer is willing to pay. They are ready to grab any job right away.

So, we deduced that an employer could use his authority to pick and choose among the applicants with no reservation or reconsideration; he could offer the lowest wage, even one which would be below the minimum wage permissible. And moreover with the applicant ratio to the job availability, the applicant would accept the lowest wage offered happily. Therefore, we conclude that the employers do not have to display any ethics and they can take advantage of the excessive turn out of **the** applicants.

After all, it is a recession.

# ECONOMIC ENVIRONMENT

## PRODUCT AVAILABILITY

Goldteeth and I left the house early to shop for groceries, before the other shoppers picked over the best, freshest produce items from the market. As we walk we discuss the type of food items available -. A specific food item flashed into my mind. That food item is rice. Rice is a staple here and there is a big demand for it. At times when the demand is very high, the sellers increase the original selling price. As a result, the buyers hold back from purchasing it. And when the supply is abundant, it then forces the market price down. Since rice is always constantly in demand, I enquired from my associate if he thought it would be available, as it used to be in the market with a reasonable price tag on it.

    My pal replied that to buy a small bag of rice nowadays the grocers would have to pay a high price, because it is not locally produced - as it was before. It is now imported from neighboring countries. I am shocked when I heard this explanation. Later, we finally see where the few bags of rice are being displayed in the market. Goldteeth picked up a bag of rice and asked for the price, because there is no price tag on it. The seller pronounced a price that doubled the price of what we were used to paying for such a small bag.

    Then I told him to put it down. The price is too high. If I were to purchase it, I would not have enough money to buy the rest of the items which I needed to buy. Consequently, I inquired from him why the market price for rice was astronomical. His answer was that the farmers who used to plant rice are out of the farming business; today's ex-farmer is now doing a different type of business, such as selling petty goods. Rice is not as abundant as it was before; so it has become a luxury food item in Paradise, and only the upper class or rich people could afford to buy rice today. He then gave as the reasons why the farmers stopped harvesting rice is because the government had failed to encourage farming. The farmers were not provided any type of subsidy to keep them farming or stay in business.

Therefore, today, buying rice is a luxury. Unbelievable! I remember when rice was plentiful in the market. Then it was a homegrown food, and it was on everyone's table. Later rice becomes a luxury. The sellers are hesitant to buy it from the grocers. And, therefore, because the product is very scarce in the marketplace, the imported rice becomes very expensive.

The next grocery item that I wanted to purchase was a dozen eggs. Eggs are also a staple. "It also was once sold abundantly in the marketplace." I told all of this to my partner. However, his face looks disagreeable. Instead, he starts to explain how a carton of eggs, that I would very much like - would more than likely be more expensive than buying that small bag of overpriced rice. Accordingly, he went on to say that farmers who used to sell eggs abundantly to whole sales-people quit farming. This is because the farmers who raised the live-stock could not cope with the cost of raising hens. Again, there was no subsidy from the government to keep the farmers in business. Therefore, I decided to buy the eggs in units, that is, just six pieces.

As we were leaving the spot where eggs were sold, I saw a place where live stock such as goats and sheep were sold. "For curiosity sake, let us ask the price of one, from the owner", I requested. The seller pronounced a high price of 30,000 nira. I stopped asking my associate the reason why the price is so high, since we have been given high prices for almost all products in the market. It dawns on us that only the rich could buy livestock to slaughter for an occasion or ceremony.

I could not shop in the market anymore - since the majority of the provisions I wanted to purchase were so expensive. My interest in shopping for grocery items had diminished. I lost my momentum, as it was such a trying time and a debilitating event, just to purchase nourishment. My partner and I concluded that the raising of prices by the grocers, in conjunction with the raising of prices by the sellers, in conjunction with the economic recession, in conjunction with the loss of the natural resources of farming, in conjunction with the negative response from the government, has impacted the cost of food.

# ECONOMIC ENVIRONMENT

## IRON STEEL RODS ON THE SIDEWALK

We continued surveying Paradise City. As we walk around, my escort tells me to be careful and watch ahead of our direction. Just as I was asking why he alarmed me, I had my answer before I finished the question. I almost knocked my legs against the iron rods sticking out of the sidewalk, and nearly fell into the cavernous gutter that is next to them. The carelessness of the ironworks owner infuriated me. They blocked the sidewalk and anyone could fall in!

After I calmed down I demanded to speak with, the ironwork's owner so I could find out why this was left open. At first, my associate was reluctant to yield to my request. I told him I needed to know how such a willful act could be so easily dismissed. He finally complied, mostly I think because he saw I really had "cooled my temper." I then asked the owner why he deliberately blocked the sidewalk. He replied, with an attitude, that he had no other area other than the sidewalk conducive to put his iron rods. What's more, he further explained that to rent a place to accommodate all his work materials would be too expensive for him. And, he could not afford to work with a well-established business man in a good location either -, since the owner would also demand an exorbitant amount of rent, almost the same amount if he had rented the place on his own.

Moreover, he told us that the law enforcement officers do not bother him - as long as he gives them a "KOLA". They would pretend not to see his lawless practice and pass his "makeshift shop".

So, I asked, "Has anyone injured themselves by knocking their feet?" I was calculating in my mind what type of compensation would they get. He vehemently replied, "I would just say sorry to who got injured." I exclaimed. He said "yes". He continued, - that, "No business man compensates or pays attention to suing for injuries sustained." After hearing his response to the pain and suffering of innocent people as a result of negligence, my associate and I concluded it was a waste of our time to discuss the matter with him, or even bother to advise him on how to do his business legally.

But, we couldn't help but leave a few words with him before we stepped away. We explained that in the past, he could not have disobeyed the law and gotten away with it. The Paradise City Council would confiscate his iron work materials and lock his work area up. He would have had to pay a fine and change his method of operation before his properties could be released. We reiterated, "If the laws were enforced on you scofflaws today, you would have to rent a place and there would be fewer outlaws doing business in the city!" We left still fussing about the incident.

# ECONOMIC ENVIRONMENT

## TOURISM

"Goldteeth, it has been a long time since the City of Paradise became independent. The city should encourage tourism by now." I exclaimed. I continued, "Doesn't the city realize that tourism boosts the city's gross domestic product (GDP) directly and indirectly?" I questioned.

My companion replied, "The city is not well maintained. It was better maintained in the past. It was much better then, than it is today."

"The city has failed to attract tourists because it has failed to be prepared," I said. "Since, tourism boosts the economy, when would the city be able to encourage tourism again?" I asked, searching for Goldteeth's insight.

"Not now", my pal answered. We continued to walk; demanding to know why in the twenty-first century are there no tourists in this city?" No matter how relentless I was in asking, Goldteeth never bothered to answer me. I thought to myself, 'Oh my God, there are no tourists! There were only myriads of indigenous people roaming around hacking, peddling and shopping around the city. This was definitely not the city I knew."

I decided to walk around to see if we can find any foreigners touring or shopping in the city.

As the morning goes along, we ride around from one neighborhood to another trying to fish out the tourists and their whereabouts. Suddenly, we caught a glimpse of four of them purchasing food products. With much anticipation, we dashed near enough to see if they had cameras or binoculars which would serve to identify them as tourists. We saw none. Therefore, we assumed they were tourists but there were no identifiable signs. We concluded that they are just buying food products and were heading home, the same as indigenous residents who always head home after a shopping trip. To our surprise, there are not tourists around at all. No cameras or binoculars anywhere with them. We did not observe one tourist in any of the venues – not ahead of us, nor behind us. Our frantic search reached a peak. We realized we were just promenading the dusty sidewalks in vain.

"Are you aware that it is hard for the tourists to visit this city?" asked Goldteeth in his vernacular. Paradise City is lousy, dusty and full of unpleasant odors in every street which we both passed through.

He continued detailing the city's negative vantage points. The city is full of raggedy vehicles, many of which remit noxious smoke and fumes which were not good to inhale.

Additionally, the city has no specific locations that could serve as an attraction to the tourist. As a whole, the city is not conducive to tourism. The city needs serious revamping. And, since the capital was moved to Idera, they have to deal with the surplus of unemployed people who exists throughout the city. They serve as a deterrent, a big discouragement for tourists even if they did decide to come to the city. Too many people are begging in the streets.

The overwhelming number of disabled people are all over the streets, constantly begging for money from anyone they see - and whoever is near enough to them. Once a disable person sees you, if they are able - they will follow you, begging in a whining, pleading tone until you feel obligated to give them something - preferably money. As a result, the city is no longer an ideal place for tourism.

This made Goldteeth conclude that the city officials connived so much that they have totally destroyed tourism. Through instant gratification, the prospect of the economic importance of tourism has been put on the backburner. But - since the city's surroundings have degenerated to lifeless disgusting place…, who would ever want to come here?

# ECONOMIC ENVIRONMENT

## THE INVISIBLE ECONOMY

Unemployment causes many a citizen to become an illegal street vendor - or "hustler" or a person who sells goods and services on the street without a license. Generally, hustlers don't pay taxes to the City. The businesses call themselves "cutting corners" in order to survive. Therefore, most hustlers engage in illegal economics - in order to make a living. Consequently, their goods and services are not included in the city's GDP at the end of the fiscal year. This causes an invisible economy that is not calculated. Since they don't pay taxes, the illegal street vendors don't have benefits - such as access to workers compensation or unemployment benefit.

Previously, the city did not have swarms of illegal street vendors bombarding pedestrians and passenger vehicles. Then the vendors were controlled by the Paradise City Council. Then most of the street vendors paid sales taxes which added to the Gross Domestic Product of the city.

Goldteeth and I are strolling on a beautiful day. It is midday and we reach a densely populated market area. I looked around and observed a large number of vendors, like locusts, bombarding a couple of passengers' vehicles. My first impression is that an accident occurred. However, to my surprise, I soon discover that the people were petty vendors pushing and shuffling one another in order to sell their commodities - or edible goods. They try to convince the passengers and passersby to purchase.

Seeing the hustlers pushing and shuffling one another in order to sell their commodities, I then asked my partner, "Why are there so many of them begging passengers and passerby before they could sell? They are also obstructing traffic." My partner burst into a loud laugh. "Why do you laugh so loud, as if someone carouse you into funny behavior?" I inquired. I asked Goldteeth why so many vendors were pushing upon the passersby.

He laughed! "Well, nowadays," Goldteeth explained, "The situation in the city is totally a matter of survival of the fittest. Many of these street vendors could not get a job - even if they are capable of working. There is a recession. Consequently, there are too many people who are jobless in the city. In order for people to survive, they have to engage in doing something - which would give them money to take care of their needs. In addition, these people do not believe in stealing or engaging in evil practices. Actually, the city would be in worse shape without them. What you are experiencing now could be much, much worse", he concluded.

I interrupted him, "What can the Paradise City Council do?" "They can't do anything," "said Goldteeth, "other than leave them to their practice of being petty street vendors. The only thing they would do is to find a creative way to exploit this situation." Even though there are on the book rules against this, the rules are not enforced. Corruption is the common cause of the disorderly practices of the petty vendors.

"It will be a while", he declared, "before a better day will come again." It will be a while before there is vitality and stability in the city's economy. I noticed vendors chasing the vehicles as the drivers drove off from them. The vendor sold the driver something but was not paid. The vendor would chase the cars to get their money. Goldteeth explained that the vendors relied on the notion that a vehicle would not go too far or too fast because of the traffic congestion. I saw the vendors chasing vehicles to collect their money or to give them their change.

"Let me tell you", my partner pronounced, "that vendors running after cars will not stop, because Paradise City Council cannot control or put a stop to the behavior. The city politicians are guilty." They're too busy embezzling and creating chaos. They take kickbacks before doing anything about it. He spoke of how the petty street traders do not care about the Council's forceful trade rules. Moreover, do you hear the excessive blowing of the car horns by the drivers?" "Yes, I do hear them", - I replied. My mind stopped in its tracks. I realized it is not only a visual annoyance but an audible one as well. Anyone could see, feel and experience this. And simply because it was annoying to me certainly wasn't enough reason for the Paradise City Council to do anything about it.

I also realized that this scenario was even more dangerous than it was annoying, because between the moving vehicles there are accidents just waiting to happen. To prevent a collision or unfortunate accident, drivers have to blow their horns to avoid hitting pedestrians and other vehicles. At times, vendors curse at the drivers. The drivers also respond by cursing back at them.

I fully understand now that the reason for this underground economy is not totally the fault of the illegal street vendors. It's the Paradise City Council which allows them to get away with it - because of rancorous political corruption. The Council is made up of selfish politicians. Their "I don't care" attitude towards the populace contributes to the increasingly existent number of participants in the city's invisible economy. Thus, you can see that it is very pitiful of the Paradise City Council to not show any pride or concern in improving the economic conditions. It is a circle of corruption; a cycle of corruption.

I decided to live and let live.

# ECONOMIC ENVIRONMENT

## LIVE-STOCK ON STREETS AND ROADS

We are strolling along the roadside when I stepped into a huge pile of cow feces and I screamed. Goldteeth laughed. He laughed so loudly that the bystanders and the people walking turned around to see what was going on. While they are staring at me, I am looking for their help. Luckily for me, a lady who saw me while she was selling apples and snack foods gives me water to wash my feet. So I yelled at Goldteeth, "How does the cow feces get on the sidewalk - when the cows' stable is nearby?"

He talks about how many of the livestock gets loose and scatter all over the neighborhood and streets. However, not every road and street is scattered with cow feces. Before he can finish his explanation, another person steps on dog feces -. So, it appears that there also is no leash on domestic animals to control them. They escape from their stables. Don't you know they could get killed accidentally by cars as they wander on the roads and streets? Most of the time livestock, especially the cows, do block the traffic for at least 20 minutes if there are a lot of them - before they are finally scared away by people with sticks. At times, although the drivers continuously blow their horns to try to scare them off the streets, they ignore them, always taking their time before they mosey on down the road. On the other hand, the dogs, chickens and cats become road kill. Nobody removes their remains from the streets, so cars run over them, over and over again until they are pounded yams in the mortar. I cringe when I hear the sound of the dead animals' heads getting smashed in the streets.

But in the old days, such animal cruelty or anything like this was not allowed. It used to be that as soon as any animal was fatally struck or run over, cars that would stop or the nearest neighbor who was at the incident would dash out and drag the remains to the side walk to prevent it from being run over again. Later, the sanitation lotty came, picked up the dead carcass and disposed of it in the incinerator. They may have not buried them as we do human beings, but people in general were more decent and would not leave the dead animal in the streets to be run over again and again.

My associate shrugged his shoulders saying that the behavior of the drivers towards animals killed on the roads was much the same - everywhere. Don't worry about it. No one cares about an animal. The cars kill animals in the streets all the time. It's an everyday occurrence. For instance, if law enforcement kills an animal in the street with their vehicle, they continue driving as if nothing happened. They just keep driving. Nobody cares. How sad. The "I don't care attitude" trickles down everywhere, I thought to myself.

# ECONOMIC ENVIRONMENT

## MARKETING PLACE

After a night of quiet and sleep, again it is morning. With the sun up and the vendors emerging, Paradise reopens. Aspiration and get-up-and-go begins to mount in us - as we begin our day of surveying the City of Paradise. As we look and see, I started to narrate to Goldteeth the things that come to my recollection. A few decades ago, as I recalled, the formation of marketing places used to be controlled by the Paradise City Council. The Council used to enforce the rules that bind the marketers to a standard of health, safety and ethics. They made sure that the inspections took place without forewarning, in order to maintain compliance and the neatness of the market. Back then, anyone who violated the rules by - leaving garbage around or having an unpleasant odors emanating from their space was imposed with a fine, with payment due on the spot! If the fine was not paid right then and there, then the goods and wares were confiscated. The only way the goods could be released was when the fine obtained either by mail or by the vendor appearing in person with the payment to the collection office.

The marketplace once had great ambiance. The tables and chairs for the vendors were neatly arranged. The sellers would place their commodities conspicuously and meticulously in their spaces on well arranged tables in order to attract buyers. Therefore, the buyers did not have to spend the day roaming around the market searching for the specific items they really wanted to purchase. The various goods and items were thoroughly organized in a way so the buyers could easily eyeball items of interest to them. They could easily fish them out and make their purchases.

Goldteeth interrupted, "On the other hand nowadays, many of the market areas are congested in disorganized, scattered-looking arrangements." He continued mention about how, above it all, many of the sellers use the sidewalks and even have the nerve to pinch a little street space to brandish their products. Consequently, it is always difficult to spot the desired goods directly.

There are so many disabled people struggling through the crowd to beg for money – yet nobody minds them. People are so unaware of the cripple that they easily step on them and fall on them. Sometimes - if a passionate person is in the crowd, that person had better beware.

They should look to the left - and to the right to watch out for pickpockets. The worst case scenario is when a crippled person screams for help - after being robbed. Perpetrator 'takes on his heels', which causes the crowd to panic, thereby, creating a helter-skelter scene for the other shoppers and vendors. Now people are being pushed down, walked on and pinned against an object such as a table where they can't move, or mashed up together where they are not in a position to run as well. My partner declared, "It is shameful that the Paradise city exhibits such behaviors".

I kept thinking in my mind, 'What ever happened to the Paradise City Council's influence?' I wonder if they were busy monitoring the market place, this could have never happened. Corruption is time consuming. These elected officials just don't have time to do the work they were elected to do and the bribes at the same time.

# ECONOMIC ENVIRONMENT

## BANKING

Goldteeth and I were maneuvering slowly and steadily that day when my eyes caught sight of the banks where I have an account. I decided to do a quick withdrawal of a few niras from one of the banks. But, a sudden thought curtailed me from doing so and made me think.

One of the reasons I was vacillating was because there were too many customers standing in lines. Some were sitting on benches and still others leaned up against the walls, all waiting to be served. I was further distracted because I saw an acquaintance that I knew from a few years back. I fell into conversation with him. "Why are so many customers online?"

Processing bank transactions in a timely manner will never happen," my acquaintance said. He went on to tell me that "timely" was never part of the serving factor. Those customers on the line had been on the lines nearly an hour or more. Yet, the tellers would not speed up the process. And on top of that, the supervisor or manager did not bother to put another teller on as a helping hand to stimulate quicker, faster service.

I looked at the customers on line. Many were perspiring profusely because the air conditioning did not work efficiently. They looked exhausted from extended standing and waiting. My pilot Goldteeth intervened and tapped me on the shoulder, whispering, and "Look at the others". As I looked in the direction that Goldteeth was looking I observed people, who only a moment ago, - had just walked in moving forward. The supervisor was beckoning them to come forward, escaping the lines. My mind quickly raced, what was going on? And I had an "aha moment", these people were probably renowned friends or relatives of one of the tellers.

As soon as the customers who were waiting to be called saw this, they started yelling and finger pointing to see if the supervisor would say something; maybe something to comfort the frustration of those standing on line for such a long time. But nothing, absolutely nothing was said to the customers. Nevertheless, the inside friends or relatives went straight inside the cubicles in the back to transact their business with the less busy tellers. Before my partner could wink his eye, they finished their banking transactions in a less than a ten minute entrance and exit.

The bank pass book is different from how overseas bank passbooks are maintained. It cannot be recognized easily by the USA visitors who go to the bank for the first time. When you go to the bank, you sign a sheet and mark "withdraw" or "deposit". After you deposit your money you will not see an instant update: there is no computer that has this new information to register the new deposited money. It will not be totaled that day! It's not until you come back, that it will reflect the transaction - you have to write it down for your own personal records. They do not stamp the book -. The only thing that the depositors are instructed to do is to affix their names and signatures on a ledger, showing individuals deposited money.

I opened an account and deposited money in the bank the first time I visited Paradise. On my next sojourn into the bank, I requested an update on my account, and was told it could not be retrieved from the computer. I was told that the account had been deemed dormant. I was told to petition the manager of the bank by writing a letter, and I can retrieve my account the next time I returned. I was able to make a deposit, however.

Two weeks later, I went to the same bank to make a deposit and withdraw some spending money. But to my anguish, the account still could not be retrieved, despite the reminder letter I had written to the manager. I showed him all the documents pertaining to the account - which were given to me the first and second time that I was there. The manager did not pay me any mind and did not bother to search for it. After ignoring me, he said I should petition the bank again. I was very upset and questioned the ethics of the banking system. I talked about how important the customers are that come to the bank to do business with them.

The reply that I was given was not satisfactory to me at all. So, I withdrew all of my money, except of course, the funds in the dormant account. Nevertheless, I suspected that it had been pilfered. This was the kind of predicament that I experienced, I complained to Goldteeth.

He said, "The banking system used to be much nicer. Even though there were disturbances with the banking operation. Still, in fact, it was not the headache that it is today." He kept talking about how, although pilfering did occur, it was rare. Those who were caught were prosecuted. Unlike today, when an official is caught, he or she will point the finger at someone else and that person will in turn point to someone else. A thick conspiratorial web was woven. The bank corporation will end up neither catching nor prosecuting anyone especially if the eminent official has good connections. Therefore, pilfering has forced many banks to close.

# ECONOMIC ENVIRONMENT

## SELLING MEDICATIONS

Goldteeth and I were standing, contemplating which the better bus to take. For every passenger that passed by - or stopped, we observed that there was at least one native pharmaceutical salesman either selling or prescribing drugs and tablets. These "street pharmacists" sell medications of various kinds, without any government approval written on the labels, to the passengers on the buses. There were a lot of these drug sellers. They converse about drugs with authoritative voices on the active ingredients. The sellers jump on and off the buses at different stops where there are the biggest crowds. This pattern continues until dusk when the shops closed and all the sellers head home.

We asked one of the passengers if the drugs worked effectively. The passenger answered in the negative. The drugs seemed not to be that… effective. What's more, they did not know if the drugs are safe.

Later, we entered another hot and crowded bus and continued touring the city. As the bus kicked off, a loud commotion erupted. It was the sound of voices yelling as if someone spotted danger on the bus, trying to get the passengers attention. However, this was not the case. It was a loud and boisterous drug salesman promoting the home-made drugs and tablets.

We listened along with the others as they demonstrated and informed people on the uses of the drugs. The drugs were not approved by the government. Buyers who purchased them were doing so at their own risk - because the drugs are made locally, maybe in an unsafe and unhygienic surrounding. Despite the risks, a few buyers bought the liquid drugs immediately, drank it, and at the same time took the pills to test the product before purchasing. After the transaction the drug salesman seemed to sneak out to catch another bus and peddle his poison to other unsuspecting victims.

"The sad thing about these locally made drugs and tables," my partner proclaimed, "is that the Paradise City Council does not bother to enforce the franchise laws against unapproved drugs and tablets to safe guard the public.

"Look! Look!" Goldteeth shouted pointing to law enforcement officers passing by. Some were directing traffic and crowds. However, none stopped bogus salesmen. They were manipulating the poor, impoverished, indigenous people exploiting the dilapidated healthcare system. No one is monitoring this illegal activity, confiscating and checking specifically the validity of the products they sell. Consequently, salesmen postulate that their tablets are legal to the populace, and as a result, the people purchase the unapproved drugs.

In the past, Paradise city had many pharmaceutical stores. Consumers took their prescription slips to the pharmacist, who in turn processed them and gave the patients correct dosages. The slips had to be checked and double checked. Thus, the patients waited till they reached their homes to use them. The only time a patient used disbursed medication immediately - was either in the hospital, the dispensary, or in the doctor's office.

Despite that, Goldteeth added that many people who used the medication unfortunately collapsed on the bus at times. So, the bus driver has to park on the side of the road and wait for the ambulance to take the passenger to a nearby hospital. Everyone on the bus prays for the collapsed passenger's survival. Meanwhile, the salesman exits the bus and vanishes among the crowd.

I ask a private ambulance driver who has stopped due to heavy traffic congestion, "Why is it a problem for people to find out about the medications before using them?" He explained that the illiterates and the partly educated populace are always the victim. In addition, many are poor and cannot afford to purchase the approved medications, but they can't afford to be sick either!

However, these semi-literate buyers believe they are being smart by buying locally made medications. Thus, I conclude that - it is a terrible position to be in. Not having money, not being able to read, trusting hustlers, not knowing the side effects, or the safety of these products. They don't know if the medicine is too strong or too week. Consuming these dangerous and unfamiliar medicines often do more harm than good.

# ECONOMIC ENVIRONMENT

## PILFERING

Economy recession in the Paradise city is out of control. It is difficult for those who want to work to get work. The whole scenario is not to be lazy. In other words, if you are strong you move on; but if you are weak you stay behind. While strolling, we suddenly heard a terrible explosion that sounded like a grenade. We turn in the direction of the sound and see a body catapulted into the air like a spot man doing a pole vault. As we are gazing we get closer, and see many people carrying containers and buckets as if to draw water from a dughole well. But, to our surprise, it is petroleum gushing out from the exploded pipe which was broken into by pilferers.

"What is this all about?" I inquired. He begins to explain that many people are hungry and will do anything to obtain money. So, this is one of the side effects of the crumbling economy and the corrupt politicians who care only for themselves.

Goldteeth informed me, "You see those people catching the oil? They are going to store it in their home and resell it when the price is higher. Or, some of them will take it to the market or stand in a corner and beckon drivers to purchase it".

Truly, I did see a few drivers who stopped and bought a few gallons - rather than buy petrol from the legitimate gas station. What's more, the hooligan pilfers petrol from the pipes - without being penalized - or apprehended. No one is stopping them today. They make it a daily practice. It's a good source of making money through an unsafe and illegitimate way. For instance, they get up early in the morning; bore a hole in the oil pipeline, siphon off as many gallons of petrol as they can carry. Sometimes they get away without incidence.

Other times, the oil pipe explodes and the unlucky pilferers are blown to bits.

The government's intermittent efforts to curtail oil pilferage throughout the nation, sometimes helps. And at times, the army and police try to protect all the feasible areas where a pipe can be tampered with. They patrol day and night. Yet, poverty and desperation to obtain money by any means necessary does not stop them from violating the law. The army and police's supervision are efforts in futility.

Nevertheless, I throw a question to my partner, "What can the government do to prevent further pilferage?"

He replied, "The government has to stop being selfish and stop corruption. If the government cared for its people, catered to their needs by creating jobs and spent the money from appropriated budget wisely and correctly, we would probably not have these problems. In doing the right thing thusly, the pilferage could subside. It is then, and only then, when the corruption at the top ends, that the nation will begin to improve the citizen's life, socially, and morally."

Thirty years ago oil pipelines were channeled from the point of production, to various distribution destinations. Even though - there was some minor pilfering of oil throughout the conduits, it was a lot less then. There was constant surveillance to prevent illegal activities, not an intermittent response as it is today.

Accordingly, oil production was enormous and the oil business ran smoothly. That was when the nation, as well as the states and local government realized a huge oil profit. Though the nation still realized a substantial profit from oil, there is, nevertheless, a profit being embezzled and misspent, forcing many citizens to lose their jobs, which leads to homelessness. They later lose their self-esteem and become beggars in the street, leaving their lives in a chaotic state.

# ECONOMIC ENVIRONMENT

## RETIREMENT

Looking forward to retirement is not the ideal anymore. It virtually has been taken away from the average layman as a goal to work towards. Employees are being retired involuntarily, starting at the age of forty, at times. Although, there is no new law' and no new rulings have been passed, there is a new wave of layoffs. Although it is unethical, it's being widely implemented by businesses across the board.

Upon speaking to workers, we begin to get some insight. There are so many reasons as to why forty is the age they start from. According to eye-witness, disability and sickness are part of the reasons. However, the universal observation is based on the view that the employers feel there is a serious lack of productivity on the part of employees. Also, nepotism can help you keep your job, as opposed to having a boss who doesn't like you for any reason and you can lose your job. Even if you are capable of doing the job, and you are a good producer, if the supervisor wants you out, you are out. But of course, corruption hastens early retirement.

As I was chatting with Goldteeth, a mutual friend stood next to him. I asked him why he was just walking around at 9:30 a.m. to be exact. He replied that he was forced to retire because his boss did not like him, because he dressed so neatly and was so popular. Many workers, both men and women, liked him.

I asked him, "Did you take that matter to the upper level managers?" He said no, because no one would listen to his complaint. They only listen to his immediate boss, the one they placed in charge. Whatever your boss says is considered true and correct to them.

I was perplexed and concerned by what he told me. I then asked, "How do you manage to take care of yourself and your family?" He says that he receives a lump sum of money for his retirement from the corporation he worked for. He went on to say it really is not enough to sustain himself and provide for his family. But, he carefully manages the money and tries to spend it wisely. He also has an occasional part-time job to supplement his retirement money. Once the retirement money is finished, he does not know what the fate of his family will be. He concluded that he and his family honestly live practically hand to mouth. I shook my head. I am so shocked listening to this man's predicament. And, I so much disapprove of the way things are going for him. We left him, wishing him good luck in his endeavors.

"You have just heard one story of the retirement chaos," said Goldteeth. "What about the thousands of government workers whose time has come to retire? Then, listen again to the most ridiculous of all stories about the government workers are suffering too. They, also, are all roaming the streets. Some leave their homes in the morning looking for a part-time job just to supplement the small amount of money the government gives them. Many don't receive their retirement on a regular basis either; it is an erratic, untimely basis."

The retirement process is so messed up. Can you imagine that many times the retirees do not get their money on time, as was promised? When a man cannot get his money on a regular basis, and doesn't know when he is going to get it, he resorts to borrowing, stealing, or both.

As we are proceeding, a man started conversation with Goldteeth because he - himself was a popular person - as well as a retiree. The retired man stated his problem; he did not want to retire, but his boss used his power and position to force him to retire. Another one, being forced into involuntary retirement!

I had to know why, so I asked, "What was the reason?" He replied, "There is a lady on the job - at my old work place. She liked me. But my boss had eyes on her too. The boss cannot come out and tell me face to face to forgo the lady." So, the quickest, sneakiest way for the boss to have the lady to himself - and not cause himself embarrassment - was for him to force a retirement on the man, me. He too has difficulty receiving his retirement pay in a timely manner. So, he borrows from friends, relatives -. But it's still not enough to feed his family three meals a day. He personally eats only one meal a day - so that his family can eat. Unfortunately, his five year old daughter passed away due to malnutrition and he had no money at the time to take care of her when she caught malaria. If he had been paid regularly, he could have fed his daughter nutritious food - and taken her to the doctor when she caught malaria. He would have purchased the malaria tablets - which she so desperately needed. In other words, her untimely death could have been prevented. Imagine how depressed this man must feel.

"Why aren't the retirement payments dispatched on a timely basis?" I inquired. He explained - that when the retirement money deposit gets into the hands of the departmental heads, they may hold up the money for a while waiting to make sure the retiree is not deceased. If the retiree has died between his last allotment and this upcoming allotment, then they have a good chance to embezzle the money - instead of returning it to the finance office. Greed and corruption are to be blamed, he reported. "Politicians are very deceitful and they make corruption spread all over Paradise City. None of them, not one, gives a damn about curtailing it. The politicians, if asked about corruption, will give you lip service, but this is it." Surely, this man knows what he is talking about.

In the old days, most employees were sixty-five and above when they retired. Those who retired early did so without much ado. However, things were up to standard then. The retiree's salaries were calculated correctly and sent to them monthly on a specific date. Those were the days when many retirees looked forward to retiring and receiving their pension.

# ECONOMIC ENVIRONMENT

## DISORDERLY ECONOMIC DEVELOPMENT

There was a time when Paradise City enjoyed full employment, unlike what is happening in the city today. Such diverse jobs as: produce examiner, fisherman, cloth weavers, boat builders, home builders, etc were easily found. Through this job diversification, the city was able to generate revenue. This revenue in turn was dispersed to stimulate other areas of the economy, which was pivotal for employment. The Paradise City Council created jobs. The populace benefited.

Today, the oil refinery has become a huge source of revenue. Oil is distributed from state to state and into the cities. Since the refineries have been very profitable now, oil generates enormous revenue for the nation. But it also opens the door to corruption. And corruption is encouraged. It seems corruption flows in the veins of the politicians. Embezzlement of money seems to be an achievement.

Huge oil revenues influence corruption because so much money is concentrated in this one industry and there is no competition. There are no other resources that bring in huge revenues and resources to the government. And - there are many ways to hide profits. So - the secret motto among the politicians is "you chop yours, allow me to chop mine."

The top leaders have access to large portions of the oil revenue through creating bogus contracts whose authenticity were not questioned.

Consequently, any citizen who is in politics is looking forward to the time when he or she could get his or her own part of the pile. Getting oil revenue money means he or she will eventually become rich; if not a millionaire, as quickly as possible. This thinking becomes a vicious cycle. But, what goes around comes around too!

Despite the fact that there were diversified industries in the past, few are still 'trucking' today. They are in limbo. Their revenue generation is infinitesimal. As a result, many top leaders, past and present, became rich through the oil revenue. Maybe rampant corruption will eventually subside one day, as more jobs are created to spur a challenge to the oil production industry is the main source of revenue right now. It is the only product which generates a lucrative income for the Paradise city and nation, Goldteeth confirmed. Moreover, almost all the politicians' eyes are focused only on oil revenue since many could become extremely rich in a very short period of time - through embezzlement and other unethical practices. Therefore, elected officials fail to use their ill-gotten money to create jobs. They are more concerned with spending their money wooing women, showing off their wealth, buying respect - and brainwashing the people into treating them like they are very important people. Their arrogant spending spree jeopardizes the country daily.

The current economic downturn is fueling rampant corruption at a much faster rate and also making the citizens aware the brain drainage of human resources as being exported to neighboring nations or overseas where the human dignity is being appreciated by offering jobs to them with a good salary. With this type of job opportunity, the migrants feel reluctant to return home and contribute to the economic development in the Paradise city, as well as the nation in general, Goldteeth ascertained.

Goldteeth concluded that corruption of the local government, along with the embezzlement of public money, which should be targeted to stimulate economic growth, compiled with the "I don't care" attitudes of the politicians are responsible for the current recession and the Paradise city's failing economy.

# ECONOMIC ENVIRONMENT

## DISTRIBUTING GOODS AND SERVICES

Goldteeth and I set out promenading around the Paradise city early one morning when the marketers were opening their stores. One of the stores was a wholesale shop. As we entered the store the workers were arranging the goods in stacks, ready to be distributed to buyers. I engaged in a conversation with one of the workers, who happened to be the owner of the wholesaler beer.

I throw him a question, "Why is it that you have so many buyers in your store?

He replied, "Many of the buyers that are in our store are not the retailers who are supposed to be here. They are individual buyers who don't want to buy from the overpriced retailers. They have a notion that they would save money. However, the contrary is true. They are not gaining much by purchasing from the wholesalers instead of directly from the retailers. Furthermore, they assumed they would pay for transporting their own merchandise in case they chose to buy from the retailers. The retailers would offer vehicles to individual buyers who don't have vehicles. In addition, retail shoppers are always overcharged in a 'take it or leave it' attitude."

"Therefore", my associate explained, "the distribution process, to follow the marketing concept, should be channeled from the original point of production via the wholesalers - to the retailers, then to the individual sellers, and later to the ultimate consumers. By going to the wholesalers, these independent buyers are breaking the pattern. Corruption is accepted by the people as a way of life all over the Paradise city as well as nationwide. Also, the majority of business people are cutting corners against one another in order to make a quick profit."

My escort continued narrating, "Transportation is a necessity for any businessman or woman. They have to carry his or her merchandise from a point of selling to another point of reselling - before they are finally consumed. Transporting goods by - using the vehicles is very costly. The next alternative means is to hire a wheel- barrow to transport the merchandise. However, the wheel- barrow pusher charges are more expensive than the vehicle. Wheel- barrow pushers use their arm to push a heavy loaded wheel- barrow. They follow the same route as the regular traffic moving through all the heavy congestion. And of course, the heavy congestion impedes a quick delivery to their destination. Hence, there is no clear cut preference towards a particular means of transportation. When the transporter knows it is an urgent job, they charge more. In other words, the individual carriers change the price depending on how badly and quickly you need it delivered.

On the other hand, years ago the channeling of merchandise was not as expensive, because there was an orderly pattern. Moreover, the price for using a vehicle or wheel- barrow was much more reasonable. In fact, they were much more competitive. The wheel- barrow pusher or the man using the vehicle was so competitive, that they would fight each other for the business.

If the two vendors were to own enough to begin fighting over a job, the merchandise owner would take advantage and dictate his own price. It would be determined by the cheaper price between the two. The winner with the lowest rate is the one who would be honored with the job. Now, however, with the increase of corruption the scenario has influenced a higher cost of transportation. This has added to the nation's economy descent into recession, Goldteeth confirmed.

# ECONOMIC ENVIRONMENT

## PETROL

We pass a petrol station and I see that there are several delivery trucks sitting there. I observe something as we have been roaming around, so I ask Goldteeth, "Tell me why are there so many petrol tankers parked idle?" I conjectured that the tankers are sitting in the stations because either the black market sellers are digging deep into their market share -, or they are on strike.

Goldteeth said, "Whenever there is a strike on petrol sales, the black market sellers always create their own selling scenario. They use gallon containers to store petrol, and advertise by yelling and shouting to stop the car drivers who buy from them. Cars stop so frequently because there is a back up of traffic. Plus, if they suspect a driver is running out of gas, they persuade him to buy from them, and, by pointing out how long the line is to the pump they should buy from him. Otherwise, the driver would be waiting for hours. In other words, the buyer saves time and money if the driver buys from them." And, actually, this does seem to be more sensible - and considerate to the drivers - if it were not for the petrol being acquired by ill-gotten means.

On the other hand, one should not trust the quality of the petrol that they are selling to the drivers, because it has already been diluted with a chemical… which inflates the volume per liter. They make it look as though they are providing an actual liter. This is a trick. It makes it look as though the driver's tank is being filled up. However, the petrol is really diluted. When a complaint is launched, think about it! Who are you going to tell? You were wrong to buy from them in the first place! On top of that, it is almost impossible to trace the whereabouts of the black market seller that you purchased it from to get your money back; or a better solution or anything. You can't direct the police to the location where the petrol was purchased to catch the same seller, because they change locations constantly. As a matter of fact, the very nature of their job is to roam along the congested streets and roads. This is quick money for them and a temporary but broken solution for the driver.

"How do sellers obtain the petrol?" Goldteeth laughed, "Many of the sellers go to the actual petrol stations and bargain with the attendants, promising them a commission. As the amount is collected, either openly or secretly, the attendant will quickly fill up the individual's gallons and then they vanish from the station like lightening." Meanwhile, cars are still queued, waiting on attendants to sell the petrol. At times, the attendants will announce to the queued drivers what the waiting time will be. Sometimes, they are announcing two to three hours. This depends on how serious the strike is.

I vehemently pronounce that this is absurd and ridiculous, to know that so many petrol station managers are allowing such absurd practices to occur, and in front of eye witnesses. This is illegal and it has just been unchallenged.

In the past, regardless of the petrol industry strike, the black market sellers were not as prevalent - because law and order were enforced and obeyed. Additionally, for safety issues, people seemed to have much more sense. They would worry about the petrol catching on fire, and would be terrified to walk in the blazing sun carrying such a combustible substance. Anything could happen. Suppose a driver - or a passenger throws a cigarette butt out the window; or a pedestrian is walking past the idling cars smoking a cigarette? Then people would suffer second and third degree burns; and more than likely the carrier of the gasoline would get killed. On top of that, because of the fear of creating a suspicious fire, drivers preferred to ignore black market sellers. They would instead go to the petrol station. Even when the driver ran out of petrol, they would wait and get it from the station. Goldteeth and I concur.

Thus, I realized how unsafe and how corrupt this all is.

# ECONOMIC ENVIRONMENT

## DWELLING PLACE

Finding an affordable apartment is very tough because the rent is astronomical. The landlords demand high rents because they feel they can get away with it. It is clear that an ordinary worker's salary is not substantial enough, and he will not be able to afford to rent a decent apartment.

Be it so, the landlords often ask for crazy high deposits as well! The cash deposited with the landlord is held for the duration of a year or two, regardless of circumstances. The amount of money deposited depends on the location of the house, and how beautiful the building or the area is maintained – not if you move and you want your deposit back.

Goldteeth intervened by saying that before the apartment is rented out, the tenant would sign a lease, which is a normal procedure, something that everybody who is seeking an apartment would do. But in the Paradise city harsh rules and regulations are imposed in the lease. The tenant has to abide with these steep stipulations, including 'no nails in the walls; which in essence means, that the tenant could not even hang portraits of their family or pictures to decorate the apartment, or uses something else. They had rules like 'the original painting on the walls must be maintained' – otherwise the tenant would lose his deposit. The tenant would be held more than responsible, if, his children destroyed anything. Even if the tenant so much as rearranged the furniture and scratched the walls, it could be grounds to lose his deposit.

The reason for the harsh stipulations is so that the landlord does not have to spend any money out of the deposited money or to use his own money in fixing the apartment. But, these landlords prefer to find a way to get the tenant to use up the deposit before leaving.

I then asked my partner, "If a tenant does not mess up nor put any dents in the wall, will the tenant recover his deposited money?" My pal replied that the redemption of the deposited money depends on how generous the landlord is and how nice the tenant was to the landlord. He reiterated again that it would be possible provided both the tenant and the landlord are on good terms before the tenant decided to depart his apartment. But, if for any reason the landlord wanted to keep that deposited money for his own use, he could find a way….

In the past, renting an apartment was without much fuss, because the landlords were usually asked for a three month rent deposit. The tenants, also, were able to recover their rent deposit from the landlords – provided that when they were leaving the room, apartment or house was in good shape like the way it was before it was occupied. There were no harsh stipulations on renting any apartment as it is today, my associate confirmed.

I thought to myself what was worse, the rent being so unfair or the stipulations being so crazy. How in the world do they expect people to live? I guess these landlords rationalize to themselves that everyone else is charging high rents. What is feasible for the ordinary everyday worker is to rent less expensive rooms that he can afford. But in the final analysis, Goldteeth added more: "A room to rent may not even be accessible. Number one, because it's rental cost may be too expensive. Number two, the applicant is vulnerable to steep competition, as there are many vying for the same room."

I felt so sad. Everyone seems to have a way of making it harder for their fellow man. The greed in the atmosphere just seems to trickle down from man to man, breaking down every man that comes after just a little more than the one before him.

# ECONOMIC ENVIRONMENT

## CORRUPTION PRACTICE PART I.

"Goldteeth, I don't understand why the City of Paradise erupted like a volcano of corruption! Do you know what is so bad with it? Is it that it deters economic and social development and improvement? The citizens see it as being the two things in one: the human type and the economic type. Goldteeth, what is your view on this issue?" I asked.

He narrated that one day he accompanied a friend to the Paradise City Council Department to obtain a form to apply for a driver's license. His friend waited in the line to be given the application. When it became his turn, the clerk pronounced, "There are no more forms to give out!" After he looked on the clerk's face, he could see that it was suggestive of something more – a look of inquisitiveness and slight humor, like a joker – the play was in; the clerk was looking for a bribe from him in order to get the application. Then the clerk said he had to go look for more forms in the storage room. He came back, without the forms.

Goldteeth then told me he stepped into a shadowy corner and counted out the one thousand nira that his friend desperately needed. Goldteeth made sure he had the exact amount and handed the money to his friend. Seeing that the man had the bribe money, the clerk quickly stretched his hand to my partner's friend to receive it. As the clerk secured the money, he dashed into another office, which was adjacent to the storage room, and quickly re-emerged with the forms that he proclaimed had freshly been placed there. What a pretense!

He actually tried to make them believe that what he told him earlier was the truth; that the office really had run out of forms. Even though it was obviously a deliberate and calculated bribe, Goldteeth's friend paid for a form that should have been free. And, everyone who pays the bribe goes along with it. They fill out their paperwork and follow the steps accordingly - in order to walk out of the Paradise City Council's Motor Vehicle Department with their driver's license. So they are each part of the problem, because no one has the courage to break the cycle.

On another note, I explained to Goldteeth - that many citizens who go overseas to study finished with a strong business mind. They wanted to come back home and create jobs in the city; although job creation is not an easy task to do. Unfortunately, it is not a smooth procedure without a kick-back being attached to it.

A friend of mine went to the Trade and industry Office to explore the possibility of fulfilling his dream-job creation. Behold the officer listened attentively to my friend's presentation and proposal. He gave my friend the impression that his proposal would be accepted at the end without a hassle. Truly, job creation is an absolute necessity. It is an essential means to reduce unemployment and underemployment. Despite the positive linkages with job creation would bring, the officer - who was supposed to approve the proposal looked at this situation as an opportunity to run a scam.

Consequently, knowing that the officer would need to know he was paid before putting his approval signature on my friend's proposal. I advised my friend to give him a "KOLA."

My friend, who was desperate to achieve his goal and did not want to give up his dream, came from a well to do family. However, he preferred not to tell his family about the bribery because they would cause a raucous which would cause serious repercussions. This could abate the proposal's approval and it would end up in a pending file, indefinitely.

My friend and the officer calculated out a projected profit where he could realize profits within a year. After that, the officer demanded half of the projected profit. Half sounds pretty steep for a payoff; however, the officer will share this illegal money with his boss.

Apparently, my friend could not afford to pay the projected estimated profit up front. So he negotiates for a quarter of the profit, which he handed to the officer without remorse. The officer stamped the proposal and affixed his signature to it. He put it in an active file for further processing.

So it's business as usual! Corruption is a vicious circle and is expanding steadily at an alarming rate. Back in earlier times, corruption was not as pervasive as it is now. At this pace, we don't know when or whether it will be abated. It is clear that it must be reduced in order to prevent hurting the economy any further.

I was just so ticked off. All of these horrible injustices are an example of what we call economic corruption – it deters the graduates who come back eager to boost the economy with bright ideas, and it keeps citizens from being self-sufficient. Kick-backs are equal to setbacks. And, the economic setbacks are leading to the human development setbacks.

# ECONOMIC ENVIRONMENT

## CORRUPTION PRACTICE PART II

"Years ago," Goldteeth said emphatically, "when the doctors finished treating their patients either in the hospital or at the individual's private office, the doctors would prescribe the appropriate medications in writing - for those patients who preferred to buy it from outside at a pharmacy store - rather than from the hospitals. When the doctor wrote a prescription, the medications were safe. The doctors would write refills for patients. He would also instruct patients on how to take the medication, how to store the medication and always remind the patient to keep the medicine out of children's reach.

This was the procedure of how the dispersion of medications was handled then. Today, we do not have as many dedicated and passionate doctors who practice these procedures. Therefore, the practice is now obscure.

Since many of the doctors have been polluted with corruption by the politicians who believe in embezzling government money - which should have been used to import updated medications, because of the corruption of politicians, expired medications are imported and dispensed to patients for their treatment. Despite the fact that the imported drugs had already expired for use, many doctors are still stingy with them. They don't treat patients with the correct doses; so they can resell the rest for an astronomical price tag. Since drugs availability is limited in the Paradise city - as well as the nation, they are stuck. Thus, the doctors give the patients fewer medications and explain how the medications should be used orally with no label or information to alert them to the possible side effects of the drugs. As a result, many patients have become used to accepting the expired medications because many of the doctors, as well as the corrupt politicians, do not care about patients' safety other than for themselves and their own families. The doctors who practice this behavior are only concerned about making money in an illegitimate matter, not about the health and well being of the patients or the city.

# ECONOMIC ENVIRONMENT

## CORRUPTION SPREADING RAMPANTLY

Goldteeth explains his point of view in a succinct way. "Besides the economy, other reasons trigger a persistent practice of corruption. One of them is that the politicians are always focused on the individualism concept. For instance, each sees illegal opportunities to hoard goods and services from the government - by stealing it's wealth - or property, based on 'who you know' parameters. When wealth is acquired through foul means, there is no true accountability. These political thieves and offenders of the law are not prosecuted, or even censured. There are no fail-safe triggers, no standards of measuring the truth in place, to establish honesty."

Corrupt practices leads the populace to believe that 'leap' (pay to play practices) - are part of a business as usual protocol. They believe there's no other way, but an unlawful government – not a true honest government for the people. There is no governing body, no watch dog organization, and no accountability committee that dares to challenge the politicians, or investigate their tactics, or question their strategies or any process to find them in violation of their pledge to the people. There is no immediate way to punish the offenders and to recover what they pilfered. Thus, as the newly elected league of politicians come on board to allegedly 'serve' the people and become 'lawmakers', they immediately turn the dirty corner and pick up the same pattern of selfishness, greed and corruption of the Paradise senior council members.

Corrupt practices permeate our cities when the Paradise Council men practice embezzlement, sweetheart deals, the allowing the overlooking of inconsistencies, and pay for play. It is openly blatant and notorious abuse of power. It's almost as if they have no choice but to get involved in the same pattern of corruption no matter how honorable they may be at the start.

The 'Who-you-know' scenario is imbedded in everything they do. As long as Paradise council members constantly disregard concerns of the common people, the society has to live with this.

Unfortunately, many of the people also become corrupt. Their thinking actions and philosophy of life changes and they also begin to value wrong over right. This gets worse as each new generation learns and adapts to underhanded way of thinking and living.

I reply to Goldteeth's analyses, "The things you have delineated are true. Many common people do not know how to improve on their lives. We currently live in a very negative-minded generation - that suffers from low self-esteem. They do not know how to stimulate their self-sufficiency. As a result, you begin to see in their eyes a bitter meanness. They have assumed a demeanor of wickedness. And they use this menacing personality to extort money as quickly as possible. They are intimidating. And they use their intimidating countenance and sinister personality to tower over others to either trick or steal their money. What they look for is a way to grab something that does not belong to them. They begin to display the mean look. It's like a formula: look mean, act mean, act indifferent – as soon as you see an opportunity where the outcome could fetch some money. As long as it seems that bad, mean, intimidating actions will win a quick score, and then heartless corruption will go from laymen to laymen, brother to brother, sister to sister, friend to friend, neighbor to neighbor. When an opportunity to steal presents itself, it's almost as if the person who would benefit financially is thinking in his mind, "Aha, it's my turn to steal!" As a result, many country-men have turned into low-level, ruthless criminals, in many cases no better than little petty thieves.

Corruption affects a homeowner, a worker, the unfortunate down-and-out, and the children who after seeing all of this grow into a negative pattern. Everyone who lives here adapts a "get over" attitude and his or her mindset changes for the worse. Everyone's life is at stake.

When you enter into a business contract with residents of Paradise City, beware! For example, if you contract someone to work on your house – you had better not pay them upfront. The contractor will promise to do a good job, and put the terms in writing, but will still not do the job properly. This charade repeats itself countless times, often with the contractor and the person who hired him argue, fight physically, or end up in court!

The problem with going to court is neither party is guaranteed justice. The judges' decision is based, all too often - on whether you have a connection to him, someone important, or how much money you can spread around.

Goldteeth continued, "As long as the ruling body and the politicians, as a whole, do not develop better morals, and as long as they do not have the humanity to open their minds to concerns of the populace, no one can expect fairness. A nation of corruption cannot and will not advance. Until everyone agrees (beginning with the Paradise council members) that the idea of 'economic individualism' is selfish; that an indifferent attitude is uncouth, then this whole scenario will lead to, not only the demise of the City of Paradise, but the national legislation as well. A 'Me-me alone' attitude cannot improve the Hope!"

As this rough mentality continues, the people who are not poor, lazy and trying to repair their economic stability do not know how to improve it; they do not have the tools to stimulate their self-esteem; or to become self-sufficient people anymore.

Goldteeth finally concluded with the question, "Is it not true that a dwindling and dying tree cannot turn into a forest? And therefore, is it also true that a dwindling and dying society cannot advance to become a great nation of people?"

This was a heavy thought. My sentiments, exactly, I thought.

# WORKING ENVIRONMENT

# WORKING ENVIRONMENT

## FILTHY WORKPLACE

The Paradise City Council offices are disorganized. Office folders are not orderly arranged. Some folders are on the floor, stacked like bricks for building houses, next to dilapidated file cabinets. These cabinets are full and with no new cabinets to replace them. Consequently, many of the folders on the floor need to be dusted before using.

Nevertheless, in the past, cabinet folders were usually orderly arranged, making them accessible, as the need warranted. Thus, less time was wasted searching for the correct files. It was easier to review or insert additional documents in them. The old dilapidated cabinets which were replaced also looked as if they had out-lived. So, there were no clean office supplies available. The workers were actually breathing dust particles. What a shame!

We stepped into an office where customers are paying bills and we noticed how the folders on the clerk's desk were being handled by the clerical. We observed the arrangement of the folders on the shabby cabinets. I walked over to the clerical in charge and meticulously approached her with a smile. I introduced myself, "I am Irepo from the United States. I am just visiting and touring my old hometown of Paradise."

The reason for this greeting of politeness is that I have to show a good conventionality if I really want to be attended to without creating unnecessary confrontation. Thus, I used the old tradition of introducing one's self. Otherwise, I could easily be accosted by the clerk if I needed to request something, or wanted to discuss a matter, or ask a question. You see, even a clerk who should use good customer service etiquette - can become the obstacle if I'm not careful.

Afterwards, I asked her, "Why have the folders next to the file cabinets become such an eye-sore?" She laughed and explained that there is a lot of mismanagement going on among the paradise City Council managers. Some managers are so corrupt that the money allocated to purchase office supplies are spent to buy a few tangible supplies, and cover immediate necessities, while the rest of the money disappeared without accountability. Corruption was not too rampant then. Yet, those days could compare to the way it is now. Later, my partner and I thanked the clerical for sharing her views on the untidy work atmosphere. We exit.

# WORKING ENVIRONMENT

## OFFICE SETTING

Early in the morning, as I woke up fresh, I decided to pay a visit to my lawyer. When I get there he isn't in. I leave some questions with his secretary, who seems to be out of sorts. I remember, though, to be extra kind when requesting that she pass the queries on to her boss, stating they are of an urgent matter. And today, there doesn't seem to be any rules or regulations about serving customers without prejudice. A mere slight, no matter how unintentional, can mean that person will work to do you in.

Since the lawyer was not in, I decided to visit at his work place a friend of mine whom I haven't seen in a long time. However, since the City of Paradise has had so many new infrastructural changes and many streets have been renamed, I called on Goldteeth who knows the city very well to guide me to my friend's job. I told Goldteeth to meet me in the lobby of the lawyer's building. I figured, since I have to wait for Goldteeth anyway, I might as well wait in the lobby just in case my lawyer arrived first.

Goldteeth arrived, my lawyer didn't. So, my friend and I were off. We both took raggedy public transportation and in no time we arrive at my friend's job street.

Not wanting to waste too much time, since my friend has to get back to work, he quickly decided to walk us through the few offices. "Wait a minute!" I exclaimed. I then cited how offices used to be set up and how disorganized it is today.

"In the past," Goldteeth interrupted, "In a big office space, the clerks' desks were arranged in rows, like a classroom, with no partitions between them. There is no private office space for workers. Lack of working privacy, which enabled employees to concentrate when working without interruption, causes chaos." As Goldteeth finished explaining his experiences of how office arrangements used to be, a couple of the clerks stand and engage in personal conversation; while others are continuing to work. A few clerks overhear what they are discussing. Then, I tapped my host on his shoulder and asked him, "Explain to me why the supervisor does not control the clerks who are disturbing others? How come lazy workers are allowed to talk- when they are supposed to be working like the others?"

My friend replied that the officer who is in charge has no way of knowing which employee is working from one who is idle. The officer is in a separate office doing his own work. "This type of lazy talk noise which you and Goldteeth are hearing, the officer may not even hear. This encourages employees to pretend as if they are working. It is not until the supervisor opens his office door that he will see who is working and who is not," our guide explained.

Our host stated, "As soon as the supervisor goes in and closes this door the employees resume their unruly behavior. The messy behavior of the employees is routine now. Many employees develop an indifferent attitude toward their assigned duties."

Before we go to the next office, we notice a few employees pointing at clerks who choose to be productive and continue working without paying attention to the idlers. Goldteeth and I overheard them whispering, "Look at the horses, the never tired workers." We just shook our heads in disdain at this sign of slothfulness justified.

The next office we visit has only four tables arranged in a semi-circle. We first thought that a meeting was being conducted. But after a second look at the office setting we discovered that the employees are actually working. The way the tables are arranged is more conducive to productivity and not employees getting up and walking around the office. There is room to pass if an employee needs to retrieve a folder from the file cabinet, which could be in a distant corner, across from where they are sitting, or behind them. They need not bump into each other as they pass. The arrangements were more crowded, and clerks would bump into each other's chairs in order to pass through the aisles. Even just a mundane move - like getting up to go to the bathroom, in some instances, caught the person sitting close to the entrance to jump up quickly to get out of the way.

"What's more, in some of the offices, there is no room for the supervisor, who sits in front of the clerks, to have a one on one discussion with an employee. There is no privacy to correct a worker or go over errors, without being overheard by the rest of the workers. Therefore, the law of privacy is not applicable," declared our host.

Even more horrible, is there are no air -conditioners; and it is a very, very hot day. Standing fans are available but they only blow hot air around. So, the employees sometimes use their hands as fans. Goldteeth told me that this is the way it is, and as bad as it is, they are used to coping with this, because sometimes the ceiling and standing fans are out of order too.

Another disturbing issue is the lack of efficient record keeping by the clerks. The reason for the negligence is that the laborers' salary ranges from level 01 to 04 below the poverty level. They lack training in organizing the individual's work. Also, they do not have any interest in their day to day assignment. They are very poorly paid. Interestingly, the high school drop-outs salary runs from 01 to 04 as well. They display an "I don't care" attitude toward their jobs, simply because they lack work ethics.

The next rank in the civil service are the high school graduates, whose salary scale stems from level 05 to 07, while the college graduate's salary level begins from 08 to level 16. For an employee to climb up to the highest civil service salary level, the clerk has to be working for a long period of time in progression; unless the clerk is politically connected. Then, he could move to the next level with ease. Otherwise, if the clerk moves up by promotion, the hope of being promoted is dismal. Anyway, with all things being equal and if everyone continued moving up the levels, there would be a bottle neck at a certain point.

We thanked our host for the opportunity to observe the office arrangements at his work location. Nevertheless, we conclude that the employees and employers show no ingenuity or creativity in their work place to stimulate true improvement. They inherited the status quo of office arrangements from their colonial master. Moreover, no employees or employers want to initiate a new idea which could stimulate improvement because they are tired of lip services of the politicians. They lie and could not deliver to the needs of white and blue collar workers. So, the workers develop their job, Goldteeth ascertained.

# WORKING ENVIRONMENT

## WORK PRESSURE

As Goldteeth and I roamed around the Paradise city, we observed the variety of people crossing the streets and we also chatted with a few acquaintances we ran into on the way in. Suddenly, we spot a big warehouse. It is busy with workers who are loading and unloading merchandise which had just arrived from abroad.

Simultaneously other workers reload the merchandise to be transported to retail stores. I am appalled at how hard the workers are hurrying, picking up the goods to reload them. It is horrendous! The pace in which the workers are executing their assigned duties is so frantic it looks as if their foreman is forcing them to work like bees. Thus, I hinted to my partner to wait for an opportunity to talk to one of the workers.

Apparently, a worker who was about to resume his shift looked at us with the impression that he could help us. Truly, we took advantage of the opportunity to interview him - as quickly as possible.

The worker told us the laborers have little or no time to stop for a snack while working. The foreman would dock them for the time they spent eating a snack, deducting from their total hours of work at the end of the day. In doing this, according to the labor working rules, if they try to eat at work, they will be fired. As a result, workers are more or less happy to grab overtime at the end of their normal work hours.

All the laborers bring their own lunches with them. Yet, the management is so inhumane that there is no time allotted to eat or digest their food before resuming work. The workers have to supplement any time that was used which is not for lunch break. Hence, at least half the workers stay overtime. Some of them work from 8am to 6pm just to make up for the "lost hours". Thus, the workers sneak out to get something to eat in order not to lose wages.

Then, there is the issue of favoritism. A boss may feel very happy with an individual's work and gives him or her 15 minute break as a reward.

Back in the day, the laborers never had such harsh conditions. Overtime was optional and paid for. Overtime was never a substitute for lunchtime. Only if a worker abused his lunchtime by coming back late from lunch, he would be docked for the time.

They are able to get away with these labor abuses because of a huge number of unemployed people hoping to secure the jobs of those who could lose them if they don't comply. Those people who finally do get a job are so happy to have it, trying their best to hold on to it. Hence, workers take extra care not to make a mistake to prevent being fired.

So, while they are happy to have a job, the workers are also unhappy because they have no rights. They work under extreme duress. There are no rules to protect them. The Paradise City Council is not concerned about the workers. As stated earlier, they are pocketing the money that should be used to stimulate the economy, provide more and better jobs. Money should be allocated to encourage job seekers by educating, and training them. There, also, should be positive human resource practices and management standards across the board. This would build up workers morale and self-esteem. Policies like these could bring the economy out of recession.

# WORKING ENVIRONMENT

## ETHICS

Goldteeth and I escort an old friend to his workplace one morning. As we reached the friend's workplace, one by one his co-worker - greeted my partner and me in a friendly manner. I was amazed when I observed how friendly the atmosphere was.

I could hardly contain my excitement and surprise and anxiously tapped Goldteeth's shoulder, "How in the world these workers are' high morale still prevailing today at the workplace?"

My associate smiled and said, "No! I am going to detail things from the way back to the present." "Go ahead; I certainly wanted to honor your explanation."

"During the early years," he stated, "the workers morale was superb, because their self-esteem was high, so was the boss. All the time, the boss was happy knowing that the workers were not stressed out. For instance, there was a worker whom I knew. This worker was ceaselessly ready to do any kind of job which his boss assigned to him. He was enthusiastic and finished the work on time. Practically - all the employees paid attention to the boss. He would assign the jobs and explain how the work should be done."

He continued, "More importantly, the boss supervised the employees' work, and - corrected their mistakes instantly - before it became a bad habit. In addition, the boss communicated frequently with the workers. The inspiration from the boss boosted employees' morale. What's more, the employees are aware of their boss's appreciation because he acknowledges the merit of their job performance."

Nevertheless, in many work places, employees' morale is very low. The reason is that, frequently, unqualified people are assigned to supervise employees who are more knowledgeable about the job. Consequently, many employees often complain about them and how he does not know how to supervise. Consequently, employees often refuse to pay attention to their boss's directives, which cuts down on production. Therefore, those employees grab their checks on pay day and go. They reveal behind their backs a 'don't care attitude'. Once again, dishonesty is the cause of the lack of work efficiency. Low esteem prevails among workers. When the promotion to a higher level comes up, it does not always go to the capable, but to those that have connections.

# WORKING ENVIRONMENT

## TARDINESS AND FAVORITISM AT WORK

Generally speaking employees give their recently hired employees instruction on their actual hours of work. All employees that are hired by the employers are often given the actual time to report to work and the time to close for the day. This scenario seemed to be an easy set of rules to abide by, without much ado. However, the rule is obeyed at times.

As we set out early before the workers resumed work, we watch bystanders waiting for public transportation to carry them to their various work locations. We also observe the workers who cannot afford to pay the public transportation fare. They are walking as fast as they can to work on time. I quickly engage one of them in conversation in an amicable manner.

I asked, "What times are you supposed to be at work?" One replied, "Eight in the morning."

I glanced at the time. It was already eight thirty. I mentioned that he is late already. The four of them are heading to the same job and all of them burst into laughter. So I asked, "What is so funny?" One of them answered, "We get there - when we get there!"

"What do you think your boss would say?" I asked again. One of them replied that their boss liked him. In fact the boss is not concerned about lateness. "Our boss knows our family and they often do favors for one another." I commented, "This is a 'tit for tat' environment."

Goldteeth pulled me back to signal that I am intruding on their privacy. I give an ear to him and listen to his warning. "Those guys are telling you 'like it is' at their job. People who are in the labor force practice this type of nepotism or favoritism, which enables many workers to have a closer relationship with bosses. For instance, if their bosses do not show them that he likes them, the guys would tell their parents. And, on the other hand, if the boss docks them for the time they actually arrive at work then the mutual relationship between the boss and the guys' parents would be tarnished. And, if the relationship is tarnished, the guys would lose their job in a situation where corruption and unemployment go "pa-ri pas-su" (work hand in hand). However, their boss would not like to disrespect the guys' families or make the guys jobless in a rowdy political atmosphere."

Piggy backing on Goldteeth's illustration: I recently met a relative (whose name I won't mention) in Paradise. She and I engaged in a conversation - regarding her job. I then asked her to do me a favor sometime during her leisure after work.

She responded that she would find time to execute my request during her working hours. So, I said to her, "Explain to me - how you would be able to do the favor for me when at the time you say you would do it, you are supposed to be working?" Her reply was funny in the sense that she planned to forgo being at work. She was going to risk her job, since I am her uncle.

So I asked her, "How about if you are not at your desk working and your boss asks about your whereabouts?" I asked. Her answer was that her absence would not be missed; because her co-workers would cover for her. And besides, her boss has no time for monitoring attendance.

As a result, I held my tongue and changed the subject. I want to send a signal to her that her leaving her job to run an errand when she should be at work was not acceptable. She should make time to finish her work and then do the errand. I did not want her to jeopardize her job on my behalf.

My associate laughed. Favoritism at work is prevalent among Paradise city employees. No manager or politician dared initiate any improvement or measure which could minimize this disgraceful, corrupt practices. The 'don't care' attitudes of the workers at different job locations are nothing new.

# WORKING ENVIRONMENT

## MAKING JOB VALUELESS

Many white and blue collar workers are on the streets buying and bargaining commodities when instead they're supposed to be at work. I engage in a friendly conversation with one - while my associate looks on. I asked if he is going back to work or was he going home after he finishes shopping? He, of course, wants to know why I'm asking. I told him I am curious, because he dressed like an executive officer. Having mentioned his appearance to him, he then laughs -. I laugh too, but not for the same reason. I put on a false grin to mask my disdain for what he was doing. To him I'm just an ordinary man on the street who could not threaten his job security. I left him, nodding my head knowingly to my partner to move on. Later, we sighted other white collar workers shopping as well.

Accordingly, Goldteeth asked me how I was so brave to ask those guys questions. I paused and I asked him, what did he mean?

He explained that the white collar workers could be rude because they figure it's none of my business why they are on the street shopping or transacting business. Many of their salaries are not enough to cover their daily needs. If they were to depend on their office jobs alone they would starve. This has motivated many of them to look for another source of making money, as well as working in the office.

I shook my head. I explained to my associate that in the past employees and employers attached high moral ethics and values to an individuals' job and the administration. Workers were always anxious to get to work as early as possible - so that they could relax before they started working. Moreover, the bosses also valued their roles at their respective jobs and monitored attendance constantly. Before any employee went out he or she had better seek permission first. Workers have to sign in and out whenever they left and returned to the office. If the employees were day workers, the number of hours they were outside would be deducted from their weekly wages.

On the other hand, if they were salaried they would not use their working hours for personal business. Both hourly and salaried workers who knew any personal time or personal business taken care of during work hours such hours would be calculated and deducted from their annual leave.

During vacation, the calculation of the workers' arrears money for the vacation would be based on the total miles distance from the individual's home town to the individual's place of employment in conjunction with the accumulated hours earned in the year. Nevertheless, if an employee wanted to incur enough vacation days, the individual worker would have to take caution not to go over his standard number of the stipulated vacation hours, as it would assuredly be subtracted from his annual vacation days. Above all, Goldteeth responded to my explanation that the politicians themselves were responsible for the bad behavior of the employees. Although the past politicians were not that perfect on how they governed the Paradise city labor force, they weren't as brazen in the manner in which they embezzled the money. The practice of corruption was less than it is today, my partner confirmed.

# WORKING ENVIRONMENT

## CLEANING OF GUTTER

It was midday. Goldteeth and I stopped to take a break. We agreed to sit on the porch outside the place where I was staying. I brought him a drink to quench his thirst, while I had a snack. We were talking lazily, laughing at the funny things we had observed. Suddenly, a breeze brought an unpleasant odor our way. I instantly, covered my nose. He asked me why. "Bad smell", I pronounced. He pointed to the sewer and said to me that the smell is emitting from the dirty muddy water that is passing through the gutter.

"What!" I exclaimed. "Tell me more about the cleaning of the gutter and why it is stinking.

He explained that formerly Paradise City Council workers used to be responsible for thoroughly cleaning gutters every morning before the shop owners opened, and before the blue and white collar workers went to work. "Thus, the gutters in the city did not smell like they do today," I asked, "Be it so, I would like you to brief me on how, from the past, the Paradise City Council supervisors disseminated their subordinates to different locations to clean the gutters?"

Per Goldteeth, "Each worker carried his own tools, a rake, broom and a wheel-barrow. If assignments were near the main office, they walked to them. If far, a lorry would drop them off. There was a dump truck parked nearby and the sewage collected from the gutters was dumped there as the cleaning took place." And by the way, gutter cleaners were only men." The women were not allowed to do that job. Their husbands believed it did not favor the women to accept that type of job, you know, for the sake of family pride and respect. The gutters were cleaned because of the stationary, stagnant, and dirty water."

He elaborated on the process of cleaning the mud accumulated into pipes that carried the muddy, dirty water into a nearby lagoon. "At times," "after the cleaning has been completed, in an hour or two, the dirty, muddy water would pile up again and again in the gutters. Individual households, if they do not want the bad odor around, would give a helping hand by washing away the dirt themselves; so would shop owners if it were in front of their shops." This helped in general, to maintain a higher standard of hygiene, I thought to myself.

After the workers finished cleaning the gutters, the sanitary supervisors would go to the locations to confirm that the job was done correctly. At that time, gutter workers were paid a reasonable salary were usually paid on time. Also, if any household or shop should pile up garbage or dirt in front of an edifice, they would be issued a ticket, payable to the Paradise City Council office. The fine was pretty steep. Violators realized the consequences.

As a result there were not too many dirty-gutters in the city. The fines were astronomical!!

"Today, cleaning of the gutters is not well organized." The workers are comprised of men and women now. They are hardly given good tools to work with that help them execute their job, they are always anxious to get through quickly often doing their job very inefficiently. In addition, some of the workers receive a subsistence wage. Moreover, the weariness and discontent of the workers shows on their faces.

# INFRASTRUCTURE ENVIRONMENT

# INFRASTRUCTURE ENVIRONMENT

## PARKING

After several recommendations, I finally get a lawyer – who, though very busy, made an exception and took my case. He made special arrangements to meet with me at his office bright and early, at 7:30 am. He advised me that he would have the first lawyer in front of me and threatened to ruin him. Around 9:30 am, Goldteeth met us and we had breakfast to go. He assured me things would go my way, took his food and left.

After Goldteeth and I finished our breakfast, we took a bus to continue our sojourn of Paradise City. The bus had been driving along for less than fifteen minutes when a vehicle carelessly halted on the roadside, preventing other vehicles from passing on a narrow, ragged road. Traffic came to a halt and horns blew. Everyone was fuming. How could anyone just stop traffic like that? After hearing all the horns blowing the bus owner rushed back to move. He had seen someone he knew and stopped to socialize. He started driving again, without apology - as if what he was doing was fine behavior.

We were not too far from a taxi driver who pulled his cab in front of another car and stopped suddenly, without minding to pull over or park in line with vehicles in front of him. He began shouting at another driver. He decided to jump in front of everyone to pick up a fare, not to park. But, he was discourteous; he just jumped in front of another car and started hollering. He would signal a driver to move his car - which was obstructing a passenger. He never seemed to realize - he could have caused an accident. Wow!

Of course, as usual there was no parking enforcement officer around to issue a summons to the driver. Many taxi drivers take liberty to drive passengers poorly. With no parking enforcement officers around they perceive it is Okay to stop or park in any haphazard way they see fit. We saw another car jump in front of cars that were already queued to go into the parking lot. Later another car did the same; then another. Rude parking just seemed to be the way, and not just by taxi drivers, but by all! So, we watched as another car (this time a taxi) moved ahead - in the front of the line of everyone to park his cab. This is the disorganized manner that adds to the parking lot's raggedy appearance.

We left the area and kept strolling until we reached a huge public parking lot. There was a long iron bar to prohibit easy access by those who should not park there (people who try to sneak in to park without being noticed). A parking lot attendant who is in charge of the lot raises the bar to allow cars in and out and collect the parking fee.

As we look inside, we notice the parking lot has no painted lines. Therefore, some drivers just park randomly and haphazardly in a zigzag manner. Without lines, there are no visible ways to indicate to drivers how to park appropriately. The attendant is not authorized to aid in proper parking regulations; so there is no strategy to stop congestion. People just pull in and park anywhere they please. It makes the lot appear full; there are no more spaces to accommodate cars. However, there is plenty of space; it is just not being utilized properly. There are so many people who are frustrated who need a place to park, who can't figure out what to do. Should they wait for cars to move out-should they leave and look elsewhere? The caretaker of the lot does not bother to demonstrate where the vehicles should be parked. His salary is low – he has no incentive. And, actually it would be a lot of work, directing drivers to parking slots all day, especially without proper lines. Instead, he does only what his job description says: collects the parking fees, opens and closes the gates and leaves the lining up of the cars in the hands of the individual drivers.

As we depart from the parking lot and head down the road, we observe that not only is the parking lot unorganized, but it also seems the same disorder prevails everywhere we went – all over the city.

"Look", exclaimed my cohort. And straight in front of two vehicles were cars parked on the sidewalk to let out friends. Then both drivers just drive off from the sidewalk back on to the street, without signaling, as if this is normal. The passersby had to zigzag around the cars, in order to continue walking straight down the road.

What stunned us was that police vehicles were nearby plying the streets. Yet not one police officer stopped to write a ticket to any of these drivers or write their plate numbers down for obstructing the sidewalk. The scofflaws get away with this irresponsible, erratic behavior. "This unconcerned attitude of law enforcement leads to many drivers follow the same behavior", Goldteeth stated. "The unorganized parking spaces contribute to the driving congestion. It's totally out of control! Drivers are looking for parking spaces to make a quick stop or to do some fast shopping. When a driver sees a vendor with a commodity that attracts them, they spontaneously just stop their car and park, jump out and shop! This leads to drivers parking wherever they can find a space, regardless of heavy traffic."

Knowing the police will do nothing and encourages more behavior, in turn - causes traffic congestion. Drivers know they can park anyhow and anywhere, since the police officer is not paying attention. Even if they were looking, they feel they have the go ahead anyway. It seems to me that the police should be waiting for the parking violators, but nothing. As a result, the roads and streets are certainly filled with cars. The traffic flow is constantly blocked because of this. All of the "no stopping" or "no standing" zones are ignored. The majority of the drivers parked in any available space they see and stopped anywhere when they see a friend without regard for others.

In the past, vehicles that were parked carelessly were towed away by the city. Public parking areas were well organized and properly maintained. When a driver parked, he or she is given a receipt for parking and when he or she returned to move the car, the fee was paid, keeping the public parking gates free from obstructions. Only in a very few locations today you might still see arrangements like that. In those days, the Paradise city council did not allow arbitrary parking, and parking lots were maintained in an organized and neat fashion. Most drivers abided by the parking rules and regulations. The effect of the irresponsible parking today stems from the open corruption and lawlessness that has spread throughout the city.

# INFRASTRUCTURE ENVIRONMENT

## IN ELEMENTARY SCHOOL

On a bright morning, my associate asked if I could escort him and his nephew to a neighboring elementary school. I immediately acquiesced to his request. I would have an opportunity to look closely at how the schools are structured. This was a good thing since I wanted to know how the elementary schools had fared since corruption had become so prevalent.

With eagerness, I followed them. On our way, I spotted a school and assumed it was the one his nephew attended. Instead of complimenting my keen observation, my partner burst into laughter, and replied that it was not the school that his nephew is attending. We continued walking because the school is not too far away, and is close to where his nephew resides. My second guess was correct in identifying his nephew's school.

The school grounds are dirty and a few of the pupils are playing outside. Not too far from them is a tent. Inside are desks and chairs arranged, suggesting that the pupils are going to organize a birthday party for one of them. It appears to be there to provide enough room for entertaining one another in a hot, muggy morning.

Instead, the tent is a classroom where the pupils learn whenever it is too hot inside with no air conditioning. Inside the tent is a big bulletin board in one corner so the pupils could see their teacher, whether he is writing or talking to them. Because, Goldteeth's nephew is part of this class, we sit in the tent to get fresh air - rather than sweltering in the building. The teacher is respectful, greets us and offers us a place to sit in the back - so that we would not create unnecessary distraction for the pupils. As my partner and I watched how the pupils are responding to the teacher's questions, the sun's rays are penetrating the tent creating a glare in the pupil's eyes. This makes it difficult to see what the teacher is writing on the board. Soon a few pupils started to lean from side to side to avoid the rays of the sun. We are also having the same problem.

On further examination, a tent which is converted into a classroom is not conducive for a thorough leaning mode for elementary pupils. I tapped on my friend's shoulder, signifying it is time to get up and walk around the rest of the school premises. As we do so, we find out that there is only one out of the three buildings that is even partially attractive. The paint on the facility is almost completely washed out. Moreover, some of the glass windows are cracked so badly that when it rains the water enters the classrooms. If the wind blows during the rain the students have to move out. We also observe that the school is not equipped with paper and other school stationary, materials and supplies. We spot pupils writing on slates with white chalk. At first, I thought they were drawing; until I looked closely and found out that they were practicing hand writing on the slates - instead of on paper. Based on what we see, the school setting is an eye-sore, and it upsets us to see few traces of the old ideal elementary school. This we cannot be proud of. As a result, we leave when the school ended disappointed and disheartened.

In the past, our elementary schools were very competitive. All the pupils were dressed neatly and uniformly. The difference today is that, although pupils are also always in uniform, neatness is not taken seriously. (There never is a time when raggedy-looking learning modalities are at cites). For example, during recreation, when it was time for recess, the pupils would only come out from the individual classrooms to play in another tent purposely erected as a cover to resist the intensity of the sun.

I summed up. Therefore, today, there is a serious lack of appropriate school buildings equipped with the necessary supplies and amenities for learning. Goldteeth added, "The problem is attributed to corruption of politicians." They defer improvement which they know would be good for schools, and focus on embezzling public money. In this way, the children are suffering, not only the poor children, but all the children. When you hurt one, you hurt the other. "What is good for the goose is as well good for the gander." Goldteeth shouted outrage.

# INFRASTRUCTURE ENVIRONMENT

## BUMPY STREET AND ROAD

"Let us drive around the Paradise city today, because one of my best friends lent me his car," I said to Goldteeth.

Who is going to drive us around?" he interrogated me.

I responded, "I have a driver whom I arranged to pay for driving us."

"That is fine", he said.

Around 10am, the driver arrived with the car and we drove off - without delay. As we drove around on, I observed that some drivers were weaving in and out of the traffic because there were no lanes for them to focus on. There were no direct paths for the drivers to follow. This made for very erratic driving. Suddenly, I heard brakes squeal from one of the three cars. "What is wrong, do you know?" Alarmed, I asked Goldteeth. Knowing he is familiar with how the driver applied the brakes, my escort sounded as if he was trying to avoid running into a big pothole so not to damage his car. I warned our driver carefully, but before I could finish my statement, our driver also ran into a big rough edged shaped pot hole - which he could not avoid because his view was blocked by a big SUV (Sport Utility Vehicle). As a result, the front left side of the car collapsed. "What are we going to do?" I asked my partner and driver. The driver suggested that we should push the car off to the side of the street to prevent holding up traffic. Since the streets are not wide and are relatively narrow, we would derail the other cars and trucks. We pushed the car onto the raggedy side of the street.

Two things confronted us: How are we going to roll the car to the mechanic? And to tow it off, it started to rain like cats and dogs. We were without an umbrella or rain coat. Agitated, we had no solution to this problem. Suddenly, a Good Samaritan in the front of a truck driver came along, stopped and asked if he could render us some help. We all replied, "Yes!!" At the same time this saint opened his trunk and took out a manila rope, tied it to the front of our car, and then tied the other end to the back of his truck. He instructed our driver to manipulate the steering of the car, so that it would not wobble in the street.

Goldteeth and I remained calm, and got in the back of the car. We were anxious to get to the mechanic, as it still was raining heavily. We could not continue like this far too long, with a rope pulling the car in busy traffic with heavy rain. So the driver takes a short cut on a side street. However, the road we took is undulating and full of stagnant water. When the truck driver sees it, he states that he cannot go through the ditch, since he does not know how deep the water is. He gets out of the truck and loosens the rope, and helps us push the car to the side of the road.

So now, we wind up back in the car with the windows up so that the splashing water from the road does not come inside. We decide to leave the car and go on foot to fetch the mechanic and bring him back. Although - the car looks as if it is painted brown from the muddy water, we just leave it as it is.

When we bring the mechanic back to where the car is stationed, he starts fixing it without any concern about the rain. It takes him an hour to replace the broken side of the car. By now we're soaking wet and it's bothering us. We try to constantly get shelter under a tree or a nearby shed while our mechanic works away.

In the past, our roads were never in the bad shape - as they are today. The streets were paved and repaired on time and well maintained. The roads were cleaned. When it rained, the drivers only experienced a few pot holes. In fact, most of the drivers did not complain about running into floods, or running into trash filled roads.

Consequently, it is heinous to see streets or roads look like a countryside which is in a premature infrastructure stage. The roughness and dirtiness of the streets, with which every driver and rider is face today, is directly attributed to corruption! Paradise City Council does not care.

# INFRASTRUCTURE ENVIRONMENT

## POWER PLANT PROBLEM

It is nearly at dusk, around 5pm. My partner and I observe a group of power plant workers parking their jeeps next to the power plant. The businessmen and women, whose shops are not too far away, see the workers and applaud their arrival. They are happy that the power plant workers are repairing neighborhood power plant. Many are exchanging their sentiments of gratitude amongst each other. This means they will have lights, not only at work but also in their homes.

But the main reason for their jubilation is that they haven't had electricity for over a week. The electricians did their job efficiently and the lights came on. Then they quickly drove away to other neighborhoods, as if they are competing with one another for a job whenever there was an electric outage.

After being without electrical power, as soon as the neighborhoods get light, the record players erupt. The buyers and sellers can see better, and the atmosphere is alive and buzzing again. This is great for the buyers; they can see what they are purchasing and see their referred choice of commodities. After the three hours, however, the fuses blew and every house was dark again – no more electrical power. And, Goldteeth and I started to walk briskly to find out way out of the neighborhood. Some people began cursing the electricians who fixed the power plant, while others resume doing whatever they were doing in the darkness.

We notice many of the businessmen and women have their own generators as an alternative method of electricity. They go ahead and turn them on and proceed with business as usual. Other business people, who cannot afford generators, have kerosene lantern and they light them. Some have home-made lights from palm oil that they light with matches. It was a terrible night. We were all discontented. Several people who are not accustomed to walking or staying out in the dark, on the street, just go to their respective homes and call it a night. "This whole scenery is ghastly," Goldteeth murmured.

# INFRASTRUCTURE ENVIRONMENT

## TRANSPORTATION ALTERNATIVE

Goldteeth beckoned to me as we were resting under a bridge observing the behavior patterns of the bystanders. He asked, "Do you see how the OKARAS roam the streets?" "Yes", I replied. For curiosity sake, I demanded to know the reason why he asked me that question. He responded that there are myriads of OKARAS in the Paradise city, plying all over, carrying passengers back and forth on the streets. They pick up randomly and drive in an uncontrollable style. They maneuver on the streets, sidewalks, roads and alleys.

"What is abnormal about them?" I asked. He laughed loudly as usual. But I ignore his laughter. Instead, I let him explain the answer to my question.

He then stated that the majority of them like to block the sidewalks for the passersby - as well as the moving vehicles. For instance, they dash in front of vehicles, causing the drivers to apply brakes abruptly to avoid an accident. Although - OKARAS' operators could have followed the operating rules laid down by the Paradise City Council, they choose not to. They are disobedient and violate the laws or safety.

The result is passengers and operators are sometimes knocked down by their cars, either ending their lives or ending up in the hospital.

Also besides OKARAS being a menace to the Paradise city streets, the operators have parking areas - where they idle until they are ready to start hustling to get passengers during the rush hours. At their parking spots, the operators fight each other, especially if one of them jumps in front of the other on line either mistakenly or on purpose. The OKARAS' only goal is to pick up riders and take them wherever they want to go. During rush hours, OKARA operators have one common motive: to compete with the other public transportation providers to pick up as many passengers so as - to make as much money as possible - before the rush hours end. The incentive is that the operators have assumed that most of the time the riders have preference for them, as opposed to the other public transportation. The passengers hate the traffic congestion during the peak hours. Riding with the OKARAS, they will reach their destination in a much shorter period of time, because they move quickly through the narrow streets. They can maneuver around the congestion. However, with this type of reckless driving, according to Goldteeth, "The riders have to secretly pray for their safety. Operators of the OKARAS could easily run into something or someone and have an accident."

Therefore, again, due to the lack of employment, many jobless people preferred to rent OKARAS to make money as their day to day job. This is one way they avoid it being idle, hopeless, and broke.

I recalled when there were no OKARAS in the city. Instead, people on motorcycles and bicycles used to ply the streets to run errands. The operators were not a menace to the city, as the OKARAS are today, and were extremely careful not to cause an accident. Some of the owners rented their motorcycles, or bicycles. They made money because they received a deposit, which was refundable, as long as the renter didn't damage or dent them. In addition, every renter and operator had to carry a valid license in order to operate it. Unlike the OKARA operators of today who may not even possess a valid license. Even when they are caught by police, all they have to do is give a bribe, and they get away with it. Thus, they are not arrested for being an unlicensed driver.

"Bribing the police is what goes on today," said Goldteeth, "the OKARAS just assume the police are only interested in how much they are offered and what they can give them." He went on to tell me how sometimes the police stopped them without a cause. Today any vehicle operator, as long as he or she has nira, can bribe the police, and easily get away with any traffic violation, without much ado. Very unlike years back when bribery was not acceptable and certainly not as conspicuous, I thought.

# INFRASTRUCTURE ENVIRONMENT

## PUBLIC LIBRARY

As our survey of the city progresses, I catch a figure of a man carrying a lot of books. It looks like he is helping someone who is tired of carrying them. He entered the public library. For curiosity sake, we go inside - as we walk around, looking at the arrangement of the books on the shelves. We observe how the seating is organized or disorganized. Then I saw an old acquaintance of mine, Mr. K, who is in his early 60's. We fell into a conversation concerning the library's structure and its composition in a safe corner.

"Many public libraries today are not what they used to be," Mr. K said as he begins to give us a dissertation. "In other words, libraries used to be clean, equipped with air conditioning. The books were not dusty and were neatly arranged on the shelves by category and alphabetically. Although the arrangement is still in place, it is not neatly put. Occasionally, when the library workers were busy checking in returning books, or checking out books to be borrowed, the books would be out of order. But as soon as they were free, the library employees would go around picking up all the misplaced books and re-shelve them appropriately."

Mr. K continues with his explanation, "And many libraries today are not well maintained. The book covers look old, are used to not being dusted and they are left scattered where they do not belong or on the floor." Before he can finish, a student in school uniform comes to check out some books. I noticed the books are vile with yellowish book covers. Seeing the appearance of these books, I wonder why a student is not ashamed of carrying out such shabby looking books but I do not want to talk to the student in front of the librarian. So, I resist the temptation of pulling him aside.

After the student leaves, I begin to concentrate on Mr. K's description again. I observe that the seating arrangements are very close to one another, to the extent that if a person seated wants to stand up and someone is in the adjacent seat, one would have to squeeze by that person to get by. Otherwise, the other person will be pushed to the side. People have to get up from the table to get another book to stretch their legs, or to check out a book. This is horrendous. There are not enough seats for people to sit in. Some patrons would like to sit alone and do an assignment; but that was impossible. There are times when you need to have several books as you are researching and taking notes. You need space. That did not seem possible in some of the libraries.

Moreover, based on this one, the atmosphere is not conducive to reading. When it is on, the air conditioning is controlled by a generator that vibrates loudly. Meanwhile, when the generator power or public electricity is off, the only alternative air is from the standing fans rotating with vibration. The fans are positioned in an open area of the library and really it just blows hot air around. After two hours the fans themselves heat up and circulate more hot air. Consequently, the windows are opened as a backup for air to circulate.

However, opening the windows can just add insult to injury because more hot air comes in. The combination of heat, all the noises from - the people, food hustlers, car horns honking, etc., is not conducive to reading, researching, writing or doing homework. Not only that, the intensity of the rays of the sun makes it unbearably hot inside the library. And the library users face a dilemma - either to remove their outer shirts, leaving only their t-shirts on, or stay for a few minutes, quickly check out books, and exit.

"Why are so many of the public libraries eye-sores nowadays"? I asked Mr. K. His reply, "Corruption has deterred improvement in the city libraries. The politicians derive corruption. As a result, they prefer to spend the few amount of money they have for equipping the libraries inside from their own pockets, for their own use. The libraries should be modernized by now and equipped with the current books, as well as old books. Yet, the books that are here are in bad shape. The system to categorize the books is in disarray, and the atmosphere is deplorable."

As Goldteeth, Mr. K and I talk, we agree that the system as a whole is appalling. We say our goodbyes and we exit the library.

# INFRASTRUCTURE ENVIRONMENT

## MURILA INTERNATIONAL AIRPORT

As Goldteeth and I cruise the Paradise city, we avidly spoke of the way things are in the present and the way things were in the past. Whatever caught our eyes and captured our minds, we compared to bygone days. While doing so, we found our way to Murila International Airport, where we walked around, observing how travelers were handled. We observe an overweight passenger's bag. The passenger is instructed to step aside, and his luggage is detained before being allowed to pass through the check point. The attending officers give the impression that they don't want passengers to be delayed; so they quickly check his or her luggage. There are far too many travelers on the lines, as it is.

There was the hum of luggage being sent along the conveyor belt. One attendant made an inaudible statement to the passenger indicating that his luggage has burst open on one side. The passenger then shook hands with the attendant officer who slipped him some nira (open money or the national money from the country of Hope) in his hand. Immediately, the officer slid the money to his pocket. We knew it was a bribe - to clear the passenger's luggage.

Right away, I pulled my associate to the side, and asked whether he saw when the bribe was offered. He nodded his head in confirmation.

Per Goldteeth, "the bribe is a way of life in this city. If you get it, you are lucky; or you refuse it, you may be in trouble, because your basic salary is not enough. Salaries cannot hold you, plus it is never received on time."

I corroborated his explanation, "This happened to me once, I remember, when I was returning to the USA, as I recalled. On that day, when I came into the airport, an attending officer said to me "Oga" (a word that represents respect and also calls for attention by someone in close proximity). I also found out this is a sneaky way to see if you speak his language. Once he knows you speak his language, he hints that you should tip him. Since he is not a luggage carrier, he is really trying to shake you down for money, but you are not supposed to tip him. He'll say something like, "Whatever you can give me, I will gladly accept it". Later on, then, after he checks your luggage and finds that it is overweight, then he can now repeat to you, "Whatever you can give me, I will gladly accept it." I said to him I have no nira left with me. However, he insisted that he will not mind the dollar. I ignored him and walked away. But, this is the typical behavior that I experience", I concluded.

"Nevertheless", Goldteeth continued again, "Even in those days, there was corruption; but it was not as easy to see. But the majority of the time when people offered a bribe, it usually is like a tip for a thank you, a job well done, or a sign of appreciation. Nowadays, excessive bribery is very conspicuous and it is way beyond being eliminated. It is almost inevitable" he concluded.

# INFRASTRUCTURE ENVIRONMENT

## SHANTY HOUSE

I told my partner to look at a woman with a baby on her back, and carrying something on her head. She's bending down as if she is tired of walking and carrying a heavy load, also with what she is carrying. She suddenly dashes into a raggedly house like lightening. Seeing her behavior, I formed a quick opinion that she probably wanted to dump unneeded materials, since it was an "abandoned" house. Yet, she closed the aluminum door behind her and did not come back out. I stood there considering and pondering why she went into a dilapidated house, which obliged me to stand there. For curiosity sake, I asked why the woman entered into such a raggedy house and never came out. I asked Goldteeth, "Is that the woman's house?"

He answered, "Yes". However, his yes to my question came with an explanation, "Ugly dwelling houses are plentiful in the Paradise city. Many of them have no windows for ventilation; yet poor people choose to live in them uncared. What's more, inside the majority of them, the floors are cemented and floor mats are spread on the floor whenever they want to sleep. In addition, when it rains, and it is so windy many of these so-called houses are blown away. This puts the dwellers in a miserable situation."

He continued, "When the rain and wind subside, the inhabitants begin repairing the damages. And even though they look pitiful, they work diligently to rebuild them to the best of their ability. They work quickly because they know it is up to them and them alone. There are no politicians who are about their existence in the shanty houses. And the poor people know there are no provisions set aside by the Paradise City Council, to assist them and provide a place for them to live."

I added, "By the way, the Paradise City Council didn't condone shanty houses, - although there were a few. People felt ashamed to live in them then. They were embarrassed for their relatives or others to know that was where they live. They looked like they should be demolished – like an abandoned home as I thought that woman's house was. Back then, with unemployment at a minimum, there were only a few low income houses built. Therefore, those low-income homes are in short supply, for those who would qualify and are entitled to them."

# INFRASTRUCTURE ENVIRONMENT

## TRAFFIC LIGHTS AND TOLL BOOTHS

As Goldteeth and I entered into another public transport bus, we encountered heavy traffic. Every vehicle on the street is stationary. I asked my accomplice what could have caused it. He then explains that the traffic lights are out of order. Since the politicians do not have them repaired, the police are at the intersections to direct traffic. What is more, some of the police officers are not given proper tools or weapons to function such as a police club. Some carry a stick to control the outlaws. In fact they have no uniforms but wear something that has the word "police" written on it. That is the only way you can recognize at times a policeman is directing traffic. Otherwise, you will just assume that bicycle riders are just roaming the streets.

In addition, those police who are in uniform attribute their lack of due diligence to the subsistence salary they receive. And, because they are not paid regularly; many borrow money above what they can repay, and are constantly in debt.

We continue to Murila International Airport. When our vehicle is halted at the toll booth, I whispered to Goldteeth that there should not be a delay here. But to my surprise the machine for collecting the money is not in use, instead a clerk comes out to physically collect the money from individual drivers and issues a hand written receipt for the payment. It took over 15 minutes before a vehicle could proceed because there are too many vehicles to hand write receipts for. In a well organized toll booth, a printed receipt would be issued instead of hand written ones.

Since our vehicles had no air-conditioning, we were uncomfortably warm while we were waiting. So, many of us used our hands as fans. Many public vehicles are raggedy, with no air conditioning.

In those old days we had toll booths. Goldteeth grumbled, "It is 95 degrees and it is hot while we are fanning in raggedy cars stuck waiting to pay a toll manually! So, you can't just drop money and go! It is deplorable!" The cars that were not air conditioned have their windows down and are just miserable sitting in a backlog of traffic as they approached the airport. Eventually, when you get your tickets, you're so happy to be moving along, you don't even notice if it is a legitimate or counterfeit ticket. We don't know if the toll clerk makes illegal money on the side, by handing out fake receipt/tickets, while pocketing the money, or if he's honest and just doesn't have the automatic tools he needs to be more efficient.

# SOCIAL ENVIRONMENT

# SOCIAL ENVIRONMENT

## FAMILY BURDEN

I arrived at my property approximately one hour before the contractors, just to inspect how much work had been done. He had accomplished much more in two days than the previous crook had done in two months. The doors were properly hung and the windows were in place. Not to mention the hardwood floors were down and polyurethane to a beautiful shiny finish. The building materials he was using were of top-notch quality.

I spoke to my new contractor, who had a refreshing smile on his face, unlike the look of hopelessness and sadness seen in so many in this Paradise City. The contractor said that he was about to repair the mistakes of the previous contractor. Since the sliding doors were not sliding properly as they were improperly erected with inferior products, he would have the ball bearings replaced with stronger solid steel. He would smooth out the plaster over the cement walls, strip and varnish the risers on the steps. I was satisfied with his work. This house was finally starting to take shape. I had no apprehension about giving the new contractor an installment payment of ten thousand nira. But I was still so upset about the money I lost with the last contractor. It seems like I am spending too much money for the same job.

I saw an old friend passing on her way to work. How's the family I ask? She replied "Oh Irepo, there are so many problems. Go by there. I have to go to work."

The closeness of a family member, in terms of caring, is abused by some family members. Many families, according to our customs always show hospitality whenever a member needs help. Whatever the kind of help rendered, it does not need to be paid back. Unless a family lends money and he or she promises to repay it. That is the time he or she is obligated to stick to his or her pledge.

One morning, Goldteeth and I entered into a family residence, and we walked right into a big misunderstanding going on. Initially, the family hesitated to greet us. But as the family recognized my partner the hesitation on the family's face vanished.

"What is the matter?" we asked. A family member begins to explain. I gave money to help a brother to buy something of his choice, but he does not appreciate it. Instead, he is demanding more money to purchase something else that attracts him. And he needs it right away. Besides, he tells his sister to demand money as well from the same family member to buy food and other household supplies for herself and her two teenage boys. The lady pronounced "enough is enough! What about me and my children? I have to provide for them as well. Money does not grow on trees," the caring, but fed up, lady stated.

The statement I made that money does not grow on trees is ironic, so I asked my partner to interpret the statement. Goldteeth commences, "This is a strong family. Like many other families, they look out for family first! In other words, this family believes in caring for each other, so that the members of the family can follow in the same good footsteps. But many times, these days, the opposite behavior usually erupts. For instance, if a family member, in this case: the brother who is the first recipient of the sister's money, should show appreciation and care towards his sister, just as she bestowed on him with her heart and then her money. But, on the contrary, he does not appreciate her generosity. He figures that her hospitality to him has no obligation. This means he fills she has the means, hence she must, or she owes the rest of the family and must disseminate her wealth to the rest of the family willingly, without much ado. Unemployment and corruption excludes many who want to work from getting a job. This further encourages laziness in families. Therefore, the behavior of the brother to sister is the status-quo, which is seen in many family settings. "So, when this type of face-off erupts one should not be surprised." My partner paused.

He continues, "Previously, families acted quite a bit differently. Whenever a family member sought help, be it of the family, sister or relatives and help is rendered, depending on the upbringing of the family, the person who needed help usually shows appreciation and respect to the philanthropist. And it was from the mindset that this is the way families treat each other. The recipient knew this type of tradition was expected of him or her in the future to help another member. Also, so that one should be aware that in the future if he had an urgent need again that he would be able to receive more help without any reluctance.

To piggy back onto this, I told Goldteeth a story that happened before I went overseas, and how one of my family members approached me to lend him a pair of pants. (He really needed them and of course he really made me believe he really needed them.) Without any doubt in my mind, I cleaned the pair of pants and lent them to him. He showed me considerable gratitude. He smiled and promised that he would return the trousers the same way it was handed to him. Accordingly, he took the pants away.

As time passed on, I was preoccupied with other personal activities and forgot about the pants. Periodically, we would see each other, but neither of us talked about the pants, even though he wore them whenever I saw him. In short, I realized that I did not stipulate as to when the trousers should be returned.

One day when I saw him, he called my attention to the pants that he had on. Truly, until he pointed them out, I was not aware of the pants. Then the next day, in the evening, he returned my pants to me neatly, with a thank you. My cousin is well mannered. And, despite a smooth return of the pants, there are still some families whose relationships cannot be equal to my cousin's example. The values and traditions of each family is not the same. As a result today, many family associations are falling apart. This is all due to economic instability, the conspicuous political corruption that is spreading day after day in the Paradise city.

# SOCIAL ENVIRONMENT

## SCARY NIGHT

One nice Saturday evening, I asked my accomplice: "How is it to go out nowadays on a Saturday night to a party? A friend had invited me to a party starting at 8pm, until 1 in the morning."

He exclaimed, "What did you say? Repeat that." Thus, I repeated the statement.

"Well" he exclaimed," People go to party during the day instead."

I did not buy his explanation. And neither has he convinced me not to go to the party that night. Anyway, the party is going to be in an enclosed backyard.

We proceed to the party. Invitees are well dressed. Music is playing, but not too loudly. This way the neighbors will not complain. Food and drinks are served according to 'dignitary's arrangement', meaning the dignitaries are served first, expensive drinks and then the rest are served inexpensive drinks. Despite the separation, all invitees are enjoying themselves. They are dancing or enjoying lazy conversation with one another.

As I walk around, I see other familiar faces that are not close to where I sit. I observed almost all the guests sporadically looking at their watches. So, I asked my partner, "Why are so many people constantly looking clanking at their watches?"

Goldteeth explained, "Because they do not want to stay until the party is over." "What time of it is it?" I inquired. The time is 10:30pm. That is all! I pronounced, before I finished asking for the time, I heard gun shots; which is not too far from the party location. By the time I look around, the invitees are bidding their goodnights and thanking the host for the entertainment. The invitees exit.

The time was 11pm. "What shall we do? How are we going to get home?" We live very far away. There is no public transportation nearby. We have to walk close to a mile before we can get any transportation, if there is any around. This is not a safe situation. We both must summon up courage to walk for a mile in the late night hours, hopefully without encountering highway robbers. There are so many criminals looking for people who work late or who stay out late. We are both agitated about the predicament we are in.

We face our host about our predicament. Goldteeth is a close friend of his and asked if he would allow us to sleep overnight. The host agreed. We got up at 4am, although it was dark. We were escorted to the bus stop to catch a safe ride home.

In the past, a party or any kind of celebration used to take place day or night without any fear of being robbed or worrying about gun shots. As a result, the invitees stayed late at a party and left when they were ready to leave. They would walk or take public transportation at any time without much ado. Although occasionally, the rascals used to prey on the people who chose to walk home through alley ways. We would consider that person actually careless. But people used to look forward to attending a party; especially on the weekends. However, nowadays, people are not enthusiastic for any kind of party to take place in the night, because of lack of employment has cause to proliferate robbers. Elected officials are supposed to help the have-nots to secure jobs, which could make them self-sufficient so that they too could be able to participate in a social life. If people have discretionary funds to spend on social enjoyment activities, it would circulate through the local economy several times. People would have money to spend on clothing, on transportation, on grooming and on invitations and decorating on food, etc. But, social enjoyment, instead, is rejected by the masses. They simply can't afford it!

# SOCIAL ENVIRONMENT

## FAMILY DISASSOCIATION

Goldteeth and I continue with our survey of the city. However, my partner asks me if we could visit a family whom he had known for a while - before we moved on. "No, I would not mind going with you," I replied.

We reached the family's house and greeted everybody that was there. We received a warm reception. What is more, the oldest daughter of the family and her two sisters got up, came and shook our hands, as if they had known us before, and showed signs of respect and maturity.

As they finished shaking our hands, the father called the three sisters aside into one of the rooms and started beating them. At first, I personally thought something had fallen from where the family stacked the household items, because of the loud sound. Later, we both learned it was the constant beating of family members that goes on in some homes. The family is living a helter-skelter life. They are ducking and running and everyone is trying to escape.

What's more, the mother has no say about the beating of her daughters. Their father has a hot temper which is easily triggered. The father thought that they were being forward by shaking hands with strangers. They rushed into talking action, when they were not allowed to make any moves without his permission first.

Before we entered the house, Goldteeth had hinted that the father is very harsh. "The father does not exercise any patience before he negatively reacts", he stated.

Goldteeth then beckoned to me, saying, "Listen! I am going to narrate to the history of this family's disunity, which had been going on since I first knew them."

"My friend and partner," he said, "Look at the first (oldest) daughter at the age of sixteen, she should be in school, or at home helping her parents and showing a good example to her two younger sisters, who are fifteen and fourteen years of age. Instead, she teaches them to be deceitful and conniving.

He stopped, gasped and listened more intently as what he was about to tell me was a shock. He went on about the first daughter and how she does not take care of any home responsibilities; that she decides to leave her house on her own; that she does what she wants to do, and runs around in the streets.

Therefore, the sixteen year old daughter, some time back, left her parents and her two younger siblings and became a prostitute. I was stunned, as he mentioned the word prostitution. "Yes", my partner asserted. "The people who live in the neighborhood saw her coming out from an elder's car, dressed like a grown-up lady with lipstick on her lips. In addition, I have heard that other people, who saw her, did not even recognize her at first as they watched her stepping out of other cars and they started whistling at her. They meant to give appreciation to a pretty girl, but then they looked closer and they were shocked to know it was her. They had assumed it was a grown-up lady. Not the little teenager who lived in the neighborhood. She had on a sexy dress. Consequently, the other two sisters started picking up habits from her. Their pattern of behavior was changing. They no longer hearkened to the words of their parents. Instead, they refused to obey their parents. The parents assumed the older sister (the hooker), was giving the girls pocket money to spend. And as the parents did not have money to give their daughters, the children's allegiance was bought by the older sister. The parents knew when the children wanted extra things, even refreshments, when they went out. Now they had that dirty money and that meant more to them than their years of upbringing and their stringent rules and regulations", he said accusingly.

Goldteeth continues, "So, whenever the younger sisters received money from their older sister, the pocket money encouraged the two to boycott school. They gave the impression to their parents that they were in school, but instead - they were truant. They went somewhere else instead of going to school. They weren't all bad. They helped other people as they needed money; since their sister indulged them. But they were no longer well-behaved, obedient, and respectful."

In the past, parents were always the backbone for their children, because children relied on them. They often advised their children as they are growing up, - and the children listened to their parents. Thus, the parent felt happy, especially, when they received their children's report card with good grades. Parents occasionally gave their children presents to serve as encouragement, so that they can do better in school. What's more, they did not condone their children to behave stubborn, insubordinate and stiff-necked as long as they were under their parent's umbrella.

# SOCIAL ENVIRONMENT

## TRACK AND FIELD EVENTS

On a nice cool evening, around 5pm, my associate and I are strolling when suddenly we reached an area that used to be a playground for both children and adults. However, the area is now fenced off. As we approach the fenced spot, many onlookers stand there, peeping in, shoving one another in order to see clearly what is taking place inside the fenced area. The problem is that many do not want to pay to go inside. They are curious about what's happening in there, but that is as far as it goes. My partner and I decide to go in. I paid for the two of us.

Surprisingly, the crowd that was inside was standing and watching a track and field event including running, jumping and pole vaulting events. Having seen these types of sporting events before, I thought this place is not conducive for this. It's full of sand. I inquire from my friend, "Why didn't the sports organizer go to a stadium? Why would the Paradise city authorities not discourage such an attempt?" Goldteeth was about to explain, but not without bursting into laughter first. "Why are you laughing?" I asked incredulously that he would find my question so funny.

"My friend," he declared "there are no specific sporting events on this Paradise city island any longer." Then, I listened to a story about how the organizer would have to travel to the mainland with the sports participants. It would be too expensive to bring them back and forth to Paradise Island. There are few stadiums where Sporting Events could be staged and done properly. The Contestants Course used to be a place where the school children and grown-ups used to go, specifically, on a day when the horse racing people didn't need it. This particular contestants' course is no longer used for horse racing or track and field events. Right now, the contestants' course has been converted into a shopping center, and they sold out. What is more, those natives who happened to know about it learned about it while traveling abroad. When they returned, they didn't hear about it again unless someone happened to bring it up.

Then I inquired from my partner, "Why are there no more suitable sporting areas in the Paradise city?"

"Listen to me carefully," Goldteeth pronounced. "Since the capital of Hope has been changed from Paradise to Idera, many sports locations which once were here have been neglected. They have become an eye-sore in the Paradise city."

So now I am beginning to get the picture. Most of the sports arenas are now transferred to the mainland. There the stadiums are easily erected; there are huge acres of land, something which is not feasible on the Paradise Island. Also, corruption, which does not seem to be waning, has prevented the Paradise City Council from revamping the sporting arenas to make them more modern and attractive rather than relocating them to the mainland. It is a shame!

# SOCIAL ENVIRONMENT

## ENTERTAINMENT

"Goldteeth, let me ask you about the weekend entertainment - such as the *"Tea-Time Dancing Parties"* which used to be around in places like Itabaogun and Apagbon in the City of Paradise. I remember vividly that the one at Itabaogun used to be called *"Saint Peters Garden"*; while the one at Apagbon used to be known as the *"Kit-Cat"*. Then, we had two renowned musicians by name *Olayi* and the other one was *Raw-Gicargo*. It appears the workers do not pay attention or are not willing to enjoy themselves on the weekends anymore. Can you brief me on what has happened to such entertainment locations nowadays?" I asked, a little apprehensive about what his response would be.

Before he could start talking, I interrupted Goldteeth again, "Before you brief me, I would also like to remind you on how I used to enjoy the *"Tea-Time Dancing"*. Especially on a Sunday at the Saint Peter's Garden with *Olayi* or *Raw Gicargo*, I remember how they used to play "high-life music"; that was the music that often fascinated the party-goers, and made them wanted to get up and dance with a lady or even without a lady!"

In full reverse now, I reminded Goldteeth of how, "On Sunday, around 5pm, I would dress up with my better shoes to impress the ladies whom I had seen there. The women were always looking forward to see a well-dressed man, whom they would try to clinch throughout the dancing period. They wanted to prevent the other ladies who may have also admired that man from dancing with him. They had no intentions of letting him go! So, I used to enjoy dancing and I always danced throughout the entire evening! Because the next thing you know, it would be Monday and people have to go to work on Monday. Oh man! I was tireless, as long as I could keep wiping the sweat from my face with a white handkerchief, showing the ladies that I was a neat person. Everything was just to impress the ladies to dance the next dance with me." I was totally back in these good old days and could see all the beautiful ladies in traditional African dress dancing the "*The High Life*"

Thus, the past activities were of fond, good memories. I remembered how the ladies would besiege me, maybe one by one, but just to make sure, they greeted me and told me how much they admired the way I danced and acted like a complete gentleman at the "*Tea-Time Dancing*". "What do you think?" I inquired.

My friend - Goldteeth concurred that the old time weekend and entertainment used to be wonderful. He also explained what prevented it from being in existence today. "In the past", he continued, "The only source of entertainment was by listening to the broadcast news or to music on the radio." Still, there were other options which he did not mention that was also part of our culture. I asked him again about the Tea-Time Dancing I used to like from 5:30pm to 10:30pm.

In fact, I remember that the only thing negative about it was the sporadic fighting. Occasionally, on the dance floor a periodic fight would break out. It happened – especially - when someone was intoxicated – too much beer, making the musicians halted the music until the fighters were dragged outside. When the fighters cooled down and showed a calmer temperament, the gate man would let them back in again. At that time, unless people had seen the faces of the fighters and recognized them, no one even knew who was fighting. So, they would go back to the dance floor and resume dancing like nothing had happened. Not only did the high-life relax their minds, but everyone wanted to be part of the dancing crowd.

In other instances, when people left for another dancing party, the entrance would usually be cheaper than the first Tea-Time Dance. People were accustomed to going from one dance to another especially if the music was not arousing the dancers, or they are tired of it. Also, when an argument erupted it was another reason to switch to another "*Tea-Time Dance Party*".

Going to a "*Tea-Time Dance Party*" every Sunday served as a great source for exercise. It kept the body in good shape. Besides, most people do not have a fun place to go every Sunday. Other than church or mosque, to pray in the morning and evening, which is usually very solemn occasion? As a result, after worship, people prefer to go and have fun on Sunday evenings, especially if the weather was good. The "*Tea-Time Dance Parties*" stimulated relaxation. The following day, when the workers would have to go back to work, they were in a good mood.

"Today", Goldteeth pointed out, "With the availability of television to many people and the lack of the different kinds of local shows or indigenous entertainments, many workers don't care to go out of their homes on Sundays.

Their minds are certainly not on going to the Sunday evening tea-time parties. And, when people don't have anywhere to go on Sunday, they tend to sit at home on weekends, watching television all day or engage in lazy talks. This is not good mentally, physically, or socially." He concluded.

"Additionally, unemployment, which has put the economy into a deep recession, keeps many people from having the money for social entertainment. So many people are not going to tea-time parties any longer, which have put the tea-time parties on hold. They are largely defunct. It's a shame! There are so many people who are not living the quality of life that they should. People want to go to work and have the money to have a good well-balanced life, filled with activities. Instead of working people, you have begging people. They beg from their friends, relatives to buy food to eat", as he shook his head and shrugged his shoulders, helplessly!

The corrupted Paradise city politicians have made the city's economy worse than it should be. They allowed greed to minimize their sense of accountability. The revenues set are germane to the economic growth, but are spent not for other purposes. Truly, the good old days were better than today. Constant robberies in different forms are chasing people away, keeping them from spending and helping to keep the economy going.

# SOCIAL ENVIRONMENT

## COMMUNITY

To take a taxi cab either to visit or to shop in the localities is a major investment. The taxi fare is astronomical because of traffic congestion. There are no good alleyways or back streets that can be used to bypass the heavy traffic. Additionally, the majority of the alley ways are raggedy. Consequently, passengers have to walk the rest of the distance once they get close to the shopping area. As a result, the passengers must have a lot of money to even take a cab, which is very expensive for most ordinary people. And, if they prefer public transportation, which seems cheaper, the passengers still have to get off their transport as they get close to where they are going because the traffic comes to a standstill, especially during the day. My partner and I have no alternative suggestion as to how to curtail the congestion, so we generally survey the communities mostly by foot. Despite that, our effort to look at the various communities won't be derailed.

I remark to my partner that there are so many diverse communities in the Paradise city. However, we can only survey the few that are on Paradise Island due to a lack of easy transportation to carry us around. We decide to constrain our survey only to the island with a promise to explore the mainland communities of some later date. Certain communities within the island itself lend themselves well to being explored.

I ask Goldteeth to explain to me in a nut shell the individual community we are approaching.

My escort pointed to the area as if he was seeing something, spectacular with unusual structural scenery. "This is ISALE-AKO. The suffix Ako used to mean a market place to the first settlers and then stayed as AKO until today. Isale Ako used to be a family-oriented community. It has petty and large shops.

The Paradisians from other areas would come and visit their relatives that lived here and also for the purpose of shopping for various commodities of their choice, or for other goods which they could not get in their neighborhoods, at a cheaper rate. The type of transportation that these shoppers and visitors used to use was motorcycles, cars or bicycles. There were so many that used this mode of transportation that it even contributed to the congestion. After all, when they arrived they bombarded the area with more motorized vehicles", he laughed.

He continued, "However, even the overcrowding of the traffic did not prevent the shoppers from moving around or looking for their desired goods to purchase. The goods such as foodstuffs and household material were plentiful. Accessories for the home, clothing, and so many types of products were available and laid on individual sellers counters conspicuously for encouragement to purchase. On the other hand, today many familiar families who used to reside there have moved out and were replaced by foreigners, the new migrants who are lumped together in the community. They are selling different kinds of goods in a disorganized way. Buses, cars, bicycles, motor cycles and the OKARAS, are still plying the area back and forth. In the meantime, the facades of the local homes are now shabby and dirty. All of this contributes to creating quite an eye-sore in the community for the visitors and shoppers."

Later, we reached another community known as OLOWO-GBAWA. Before my partner could delineate how the community used to be, I was shocked at not being about to recognize the area. It was transformed from its original modern makeup to an archaic look. The structures of the homes were different. Then Goldteeth stated it used to be a family-oriented neighborhood as well as a commercial area. I used to have a well renowned movie theater, the Ralto. It had top rated movies. People from all over would come to watch the movies there. It was very crowded there on the weekends.

I responded sadly, "One of my relatives used to have a shop for selling stock fish imported from Iceland here; and adjacent to his store was a grocery store. There was a restaurant where many white and blue collar workers are during their lunch hours. There were so many shops. There was plenty of competition. Some of the shops used to entertain the shoppers and diners with high life music. At times, you would hear "traditional" music echoing with talking drums in the background as you perused the area. People who had an affinity for it would dance to it, regardless of day or evening.

It was sad to see that so many land-marks such as the *Ralto Cinema* had disappeared. The other things that were demolished were the homes, shops, and petty entertainment stores, other renowned landmarks to create room for an overpass, which extended from the IDDA Shopping area, which ran and passed through the community. Nowadays pedestrians, petty traders, squatters and human congestion occupy the area. Therefore, the old days have almost vanished from the people who used to live here. Those who passed on are now forgotten because of the political corruption.

"Goldteeth, where are we now?" I inquired. "You don't remember this locality?" It hit me! "Yes. This is the Kampo Square Community which used to be known as Brazilian quarters. The people were the Hopens who migrated back to Hope after slavery was abolished, and settled there." But, in my mind's eye, I realized there were many landmarks which were no longer there.

Goldteeth told me that landmarks are gone or relocated, such as Baatis Academy, a high school; and Methodi Girls' High School grounds. I remembered a location in the Kampo known as Kampo Square where many rascals used to plan how they would disgrace any girl or lady who were arrogant when passing, or who did not show respect for any of the members. As a result, most of the ladies who don't want to be disturbed passed through another street to avoid harassment.

In the day and the evening, there was a record shop where a variety of music was played for those who were interested in purchasing them. When *the highlife music was being played* especially the popular ones, the boys and girls would dance showing their individual skills on a particular tune. They demonstrated how to dance to it correctly.

I used to live in the neighborhood and would stop to enjoy the latest records. One night, a guy there was dancing and sweating excessively. The record stopped, perhaps because he was the second best dancer. Suddenly, less than a minute later the dancer collapsed because his blood was frozen and he died - as he finished drinking iced water. Within five minutes, everyone vanished like lightening because they did not want to be called by the police as eye witnesses. I felt so sorry for the guy's sudden passing. We learned later about drinking icy water. I wished a knowledgeable person had been around to advise the dancer not to drink very ice cold water while he was sweating so profusely.

Today, few of the landmarks still remain, such as, Katadira Church which is on Katalik Mission Street and Police Headquarters. There is a new high school called Ako High School that recently has been built. The disappearance of so many landmarks is influenced by the constant corruption of the politicians in the Paradise city. Money is not spent for revitalizing the deteriorated landmarks and buildings, or for the historical tombs and the police headquarters. Even the new Paradise City Council building, which was recently built, looks centuries old and almost deteriorated. Some of the windows are cracked and later fixed and the paint on the building at times is fading.

# SOCIAL ENVIRONMENT

## FAMILIARITY FALLS APART

One cool evening, I called on my partner to take a walk to stop at a friends' place.

As we stroll along a popular street named - *Inandi Asikiwe*, we sighted an old friend of mine whom I haven't seen for a long time. My friend recognized him as well. We walk to where he sat, majestically. He shook our hands and sat down quietly - without asking us to sit or to look for a bench where we could sit to keep his company. Since he didn't offer us a seat, we did not even suggest to him to take us to his apartment to say hello to his family. Consequently, we both still stood in front of him like a log of wood, talking to him to maintain courtesy. Meanwhile, he appeared to be tired of our friendly discussion with him and says, "I will be talking with you at another time and he left us." Still standing there, my partner and I looked at one another as he walked away.

I could hardly hold my tongue, "Why did our old friend behave very cold to both of us?" Goldteeth stated that many friends that he knows are not willing to interact very closely because they are afraid to suggest to offer you a drink or to ask you to come in to have food. The reason for the appearance of unconcern of unfriendliness or lack of hospitality is because of lack of job or severe poverty. My friends are struggling to have even a single meal a day. And, as for the friends who are retired, they don't get their retirement money in a timely manner. So, they cannot afford to entertain their own relatives.

"Goldteeth", I replied, "Your explanation regarding the unfriendliness of many friends in the city today reminds me of a friend that both of us used to go out with frequently - before I traveled overseas. This friend as well went overseas and when he returned he could not get a job, any job. So he now stays home and is idle. He started to hustle seriously every day to survive. I happened to see him regularly with my cousin who knew his whereabouts. Once I ran into him unexpectedly - with my cousin. He told my cousin to bring me to his residence whenever I decided to pay him a visit. When I asked him, he would not even give me his cellular number to call him, so that I would not just visit him unannounced."

"The following day, my cousin came to pick me up and straight away we arrived at his residence". Where my friend lives is not strange to my cousin. My cousin first spoke to a guy who lived in the same building and knew him very well. He told him that my friend had just got home a few minutes ago. Filled with curiosity, I urged my cousin to let us go to his apartment, so that we could have more time to chat with him. Behold, my cousin knocked at his apartment door and we expected the door to open because we could hear his radio on; also we heard his footsteps. My cousin knocked constantly. Maybe he did not hear the first knock; yet the door is not opened. As a result, my cousin went back to the mate's apartment to inquire again whether my old friend is truly in this apartment. The man said, "Yes, he is in his apartment." Again, in order not to be a nuisance, my cousin called my old friend's name and we appeared to leave the premises. Instead of us leaving completely, however, we hid a block away - so we could see the residents coming and going from the building. At last, we saw my old friend coming out and walking towards where we are hidden. As he was about to pass us, my cousin called him. He looked at us as if something bothered him. And he did not talk to or greet us. Instead, he kept going." At this moment, Goldteeth smiled and said to me that he is a bad friend. It is a common practice for a friend to duck from a friend these days.

Nevertheless, Goldteeth said to me that in the past friends used to be friends and they appreciated each other. Whenever friends see friends, they are ready to entertain one another, without much fuss. In addition, in those days, friends were always glad to render help to one another. Unlike today, friends often act like they don't care about friends as much, in order to prevent unexpected expenses.

# SOCIAL ENVIRONMENT

## WHICH POLITICIAN IS RIGHT OR WRONG?

"Goldteeth, how do you see our politicians nowadays?" I asked. His reply was very interesting indeed. "The majority of them have turned a good leaf into a bad leaf. In other words, these politicians only look at their pockets, friends and cohorts. These politicians cannot be relied on - or trusted. Hence, it is very hard for the populace to consistently determine which one of them is right or wrong, when it comes to how to create a best approach to revitalizing Paradise City and the hullabaloo (confusion) in the Paradise city continuously."

I insisted on hearing more of his views about the politicians, so he further revealed. "There are very few dedicated political leaders who could successfully handle the pros and cons, or could reduce the economic chaos, such as, the good times or bad times which the paradise inhabitants are enduring every day. For instance, whenever they observe that many people are out of work, instead of putting their heads together to create a variety of jobs as their priority, many of them connived instead and made the lives of the people even more miserable. Whereby, as a result, hoodlums develop constant ways of stealing from the haves and the have-nots; to the extent they are highway robbers and are increasing, and they could not be wiped out. Thus, crime is constantly escalating, at a daily rate. Consequently, people's daily lives are always at risk. It's a shame."

I recalled that when I used to live in Paradise, politicians were more refined. That is, they always consulted among themselves to see who would better serve or be more passionate to the needs of the Paradise city. The voters could speak well of the individuals. At the time, they made sure they fulfilled whatever they promised the voter without much ado. Furthermore, these politicians were at least trustworthy.

# DEMOGRAPHIC ENVIRONMENT

# DEMOGRAPHIC ENVIRONMENT

## AREA POPULATION

I met with my new lawyer, Casim Billo so early in the morning, 7 am. It was a beautiful dawn in Paradise City. He explained to me what steps he had already taken. After surveying the building and land, he went to the Land Reacquisition Unit for the actual tax cost, all before going for the issuing of the COO (Certificate of occupancy). I thought to myself, Billo resubmitted the documents correctly, in the right order, (as the previous lawyer had submitted the COO paperwork but without getting the figures on the taxation first). I asked Billo, "Why didn't the other lawyer do it this way?" He said, "Your other lawyer, the one called Joyee Kuya was ignorant pertaining to the ways and procedures that it takes to get a Certificate of Occupancy. Of course, he should have gone to the Land Reacquisition section to inquire first and then get the actual tax cost before going for the issuing of the COO, and before going to the COO office. By doing the opposite, he made the file dormant for a long time in the unit with lack of proper actions."

I stood there taking it all in. Although that other low-life Kuya had actually done some work, he just did not understand the proper steps – he was so incompetent. And, of course on top of everything, he was a thief. He was just a conniving, sham-lawyer who embezzled part of my money.

I gave my new good lawyer Billo a large sum of money. I even gave him extra, just in case of an unexpected KOLA payment. Even a decent honest lawyer has to pay the piper; since KOLA has now been accepted as a part of business practice. Nevertheless, I feel confident about what he is doing - even though the money, the costs have now risen to a ridiculous amount.

As I walked away after shaking his hand, I couldn't help but think about Kuya. He was a just a low-down crook. I had wasted all of the contingency money with him. I wanted that money back. But I realized it would be an uphill battle to get it back. In a court of law, how could I prove that I gave that lying Kuya extra money for KOLA and that he should return it? It would be my word against his, and I would lose anyway. You can't fight an illegal money transaction in court.

I guess all is well that ends well, although it wasn't final yet. I just felt better. After talking with Billo, I felt so much relief in my business dealings. I decided to go back to the place I was staying, eat a bit, and take a one hour nap. I was exhausted!

On this bright sunny day, after having rested till midday, I woke up refreshed and ready to continue my exploration. Goldteeth and I are walking. I asked Goldteeth, if he does not mind to stop and pray. I had been feeling so down, having been ripped off financially by my old lawyer and old contractor. I was seeking a divine intervention. I had seen so much negativity in the Paradise city, and before we started our day, I thought this would help. "Maybe we will have a more spiritual path today," I told Goldteeth.

Goldteeth begins to pray and before ending the prayer, he just started to talk again, "Irepo, my friend, from Iduma through the Itabaogun area, it is roughly estimated that there are approximately 100,000 people shopping. This number represents people who are walking around, the peddlers, hustlers, the physically challenged, cyclists and trucks (lorry) which occasionally obstruct the free movements of people."

"This is a huge crowd of people," I ascertained. "Why do so many people choose to shop in these two localities?" I asked. He didn't answer me; but it was okay since I really wanted to just keep walking. I observed however, that it was also quite an inconvenience for the people to shop in these crowded vicinities. And, I wanted to observe for myself what the ramifications were. We keep on walking.

As it's an extremely hot day and I am wearing my sunglasses, through them I see very vividly that the women outnumber the men. I mention this to my partner. "You are correct," my associate confirmed, "but the bigger picture is that there are too many people overall." This was the truth, there were other ways too for many people buying and bargaining for the items of their choice. What's more, the people are rude. They have no patience and are pushing others like the wind blowing effigies erected to scare away birds which are about to destroy the corn cubs on the stalks planted in the farm. Several times, we had to halt to allow people to pass by.

Within a few seconds, an altercation erupted. The crowd dispersed and started running helter-skelter when enemies invade a village. Instead of panicking like the crowd, we dashed into a nearby shop to take cover, until the commotion subsided. As the midday sun takes its toll on the crowd, we decided to rest in an alley way covered with tents. To our surprise, it appeared we moved from "the frying pan into the fire", as the alley was filled with another big crowd so much so that we instantly changed lanes like a race car driver who is about to run into a pit. "This is terrible," my partner pronounced. I echoed him right away.

Looking around as we mixed with the crowd, many sellers laid their commodities along the sidewalks, creating more congestion. The sellers have to bend over to look at their goods, to prevent the crowd from stepping on the goods, and to make the shoppers aware that they are the sellers standing next to their commodities. What a strenuous and stressful shopping locality. This is it, I thought to myself. Many of the sellers are sweating, and wiping their faces, and at the same time they are watching over their goods for another reason – to make sure they are not stolen (as the crowd is moving like the locusts on the streets).

"Is this how Itabaogun and Iduma used to be congested with people?" I demanded.

"No." my associate replied.

"Then explain how both places used to be?" I needed to know.

"Well, the population of the shoppers and others used to be light in comparison to what it is today." Goldteeth started describing the past, "The numbers of shoppers back then was roughly 20,000 around midday. Including the workers who were on their lunch hours, the men and women ran around briskly. Some came with their kids doing their shopping as quickly as possible. Because the goods were well laid out, the sidewalks and streets were clean and were not bombarded with crowds. About three-quarters of the crowd then were actually women who were the shop owners. The men were only about a quarter" he concluded, as he thought back, surveying a picture in his mind. He also added that there were few migrants, in the Paradise city, usually in the low hundreds; unlike today when the migrant population is in the thousands.

The cause for the enormous migration to the Paradise city is because oil is being dispensed from Paradise to overseas from crude oil production plants. Because of the huge demand of the crude oil overseas, and the fact that we have an abundant supply, workers realize huge salaries and wages. Consequently, people who used to be farmers, unemployed from the interior have rushed to Paradise City with the intention of getting a job and "keeping up with the Jones's"

However, the excessive migration to the Paradise city made the city over populated. The fact that the migrants would not return to their respective towns or cities, there is over crowding in Paradise City. Since - they have tasted a higher standard of living, and they refused to go back home for fear of becoming nuisances in their home towns or cities. Thus, they decided to hang around here instead and be an even bigger nuisance in their newly adopted town.

# DEMOGRAPHIC ENVIRONMENT

## IFA BELIEF

The Ifa Deity that we are examining is derived from the Yoruba mythology. So, our description of it will not deal with the data aspects of the DEMOGRAPHIC.

Goldteeth, let me tell you, "no human being, now or then could live without a belief in something! In God, or being conceived as the perfect, omnipotent, omniscient originator and ruler of the universe or some principal object of faith and worship is what they call monotheistic religions." Here, one of the focused beliefs back in the days was the Ifa Oracle, the God of wisdom in whom the worshippers believed that their prayers would only be heard from Ifa through God. Ifa Oracle is a shrine consecrated as a prophetic deity, many of our people strongly hearkened and stuck to the prophetic deity with its frequent predictions and forecasts. Ifa is not only practiced in the City of Paradise, but its practice also disseminated throughout the Yoruba territories. Many of its members wear white attire, shoes or slippers, assorted colored beads round their neck and carry white Iruke (oxtail) in their hands for recognition. Whenever the member performs an outside ceremony, it is usually done on a Wednesday for it.

The Ifa Oracle followers usually wear white clothes and assorted colored beads. They beat bells with a stick, and dance. This is often dedicated to worship and praise of the prophetic deity in the Ile-Awo or (synagogue). The worship is often echoed with the beating of the iron bells during the singing.

We observed a ceremony one pleasant evening - when it was less humid and much more comfortable. When my friend and I are promenading along an area called Isale-Ako, I heard loud singing. I became very excited and instantly inquired from Goldteeth the purpose for the singing and the iron bells which reverberated through the night? Not to waste time in explaining the purpose of the noises, my friend dragged me hastily to the location of members' ritual performances where words of incantations were being recited.

To our surprise, the outside onlookers who gathered were very respectful. We did not notice any unusual gestures from the IfA priests which would warrant laughing, or be viewed as entertainment. So there was no clapping from any of the spectators. The spectators were quite, very respectful watching how the rituals are being performed. According to my friend, "No one could laugh at them, should there be a case where laughable gestures are displayed. It would reflect a sigh of disrespect for their deity. Besides, whoever deemed it necessary to laugh would be cursed forever and the end result can have serious, life threatening consequences. There is nothing to laugh about here!"

Since we are in the midst of many onlookers, we could not penetrate the spectators to "poke – nose" deeper so that maybe we could observe things better. However, all the onlookers are barricaded, which is ten yards back so they could not crowd the ceremonies. Unlike the past days, the onlookers often got too close to the members. Although they want to observe the activities of the members, it often became too close for comfort. The members had to use their hands to push the spectators from disturbing them.

On the other hand, today there are not too many believers in Ifa deity. Many of the members pulled out and converted to Christianity or the Muslim faith. And, unfortunately, the younger generation is not at all fascinated with the Ifa Oraacle. Due to corruption practices again, our children have lost their culture. Part of the reason for the disorderly of our children can be contributed to their loss of identity, tradition, and the respect for the religions of their elders. Besides, the young generation parents who do not allow them to be influenced by the members do not understand they are killing their own culture. Therefore, the rituals performances on Wednesday are often slated for tourists.

# DEMOGRAPHIC ENVIRONMENT

## CULTURAL BELIEFS

The cultural beliefs are deduced from the Mythology. And we would focus on its aspect which deals with the religious beliefs. There are two major groups that stress the religious beliefs. They are the Muslim and the Christian beliefs. Furthermore, we are going to stress the individuals' religious beliefs regarding how they educate our youth.

I asked my partner to explain differences between the two major outside religious, Muslim and Christianity, concerning sending their young ones to school. Goldteeth started with the Muslim view first. "Let us visit an Arabic school to observe the basis of the Muslims' doctrines." "Look!" My partner tapped me on my shoulder and asked me if I could guess the ages of the kids that are learning Arabic right now.

I immediately told him that the age starts, I guess, from 5 and above. Then I asked him, "Why are there so many young children and only a few grownups?"

Then, my associate revealed that the Muslims put a major emphasis on Arabic language. Thus, they prefer to send their children to learn Arabic first and later to western schools provided for the kids. Parents are convinced that their children will master the Arabic language. Later, the parents allow their children to go to school in the evening to attend Arabic classes. Or, the parents could restrict their children to finish their Arabic lessons first, before sending them to school.

What is the implication of sending the kids to learn Arabic first when they should have been in the western culture schools since their brains are fresh enough to grasp things that are being taught in the school? His reply to the question is that the Muslims wanted their children to know more about the prophet Mohammed. So, they emphasize the Arabic language and being able to interpret the Koran. The youth would only know more about the prophet through learning the Arabic language in the Koran. As a result, a parent would be very happy if their child became an Imam, or a teacher, teaching the language itself. Still, the parents also believed that in case their children wanted to go to the western culture school, the children would pick up the Christian doctrines, which are always attributed to the western culture.

Hence, the children would lose the hope of learning the Arabic language even if he took it after they graduated from the Christian school. They would prone to the western school culture instead, or the Muslims doctrines. Also, Muslims do not want their girls to be well educated; since they would be exposed to corruption before their age of puberty. Muslims' population in the Paradise city is roughly 60 percent!

On the other hand, Christianity stems from the western culture, through which the Christians believe that their children would develop knowledge faster if they go to the Christian schools at an early age, and flow with the western culture. They could become important people in the future, provided the children go to school early, say, from the age of 5 and above and focus on learning.

Goldteeth and I reached a school where many of the pupils were from Christians' homes. They were in different grades and classrooms. However, one class focused on teaching from the bible, the Christian doctrines relating to the birth of Jesus and how he was crucified on the cross.

We entered into another class where teaching social studies was being covered; and in another class a teacher was teaching science. Time passed quickly. It was time to go home. My partner and I left with the school crowd. Christians are 40 percent of the population in Paradise.

It is assumed that Christians prefer sending their children to western schools, as opposed to the Muslim schools because their children will get good jobs, provided they graduate from the school. Also, the children would not become illiterate in their youth if they go to school. Christian children who follow Jesus' doctrines when young will not be persuaded to other religions, as adults.

Goldteeth stressed that both the Muslims and Christians relaxed their perception on beliefs by sending their kids to the parents' dominant cultural school settings. Today, the Muslims or Christians focus mainly on their doctrines. Otherwise, the kids could have easily refused to go to any of the religious schools. My partner, therefore, restated that the two major religious cultures between the Muslims and the Christians have blended, especially in the restrictive areas and are no more taken seriously.

# DEMOGRAPHIC ENVIRONMENT

## HABITUAL PRACTICE

Goldteeth and I were ambling around one of the popular squares when we heard a sound ARA-OKE bouncing off the walls. I anxiously looked toward the direction that it was coming from. I asked my associate, "What does that mean?"

My associate smiled in a disarming manner as if to put me at ease.

According to Goldteeth, the word ARA-OKE is attributed to people who are born and bred in the interior. People who were born outside of the Paradise localities speak with an accent that does not conform with the Paradisians accent.

The word is also viewed as a pejorative whenever it is addressed towards a person. Furthermore, it signifies a blatant stigma whose interpretation of average Paradisians is more exotic in nature and as well as the interior migrants.

As we continue to walk, we reach an open shaded area partially covered by trees. We overhear a group of people with accents discoursing among themselves.

I quickly signal to my cohort to pretend we are resting under the tree shade - so we could listen to their accents.

Within minutes, two guys passed close to where the group is talking. One person in the group happened to know one of them and yelled ARA-OKE. It is then that I believed that any person who does not speak like the people who are residing in Paradise would automatically stigmatize the word; also if they have facial tribal marks.

As we departed from the area near the group and walked about three blocks, we ran into two friends. My friend Goldteeth tapped them purposely to point out tribal marks on their faces, which indicated that Paradise residents who saw their tribal marks would instantly call the two the ARA-OKES.

"It is a shame," my associated commented, "that such a word is also frequently being used to identify a person who has tribal marks - within the Yoruba tribe." Anyway, the ARA-OKE is less used today. There is a lot of inter-marriage going on between the people with the tribal marks on their faces, so the negative implication is fading out slowly and steadily as corruption speeds up intermarriages.

# DEMOGRAPHIC ENVIRONMENT

## MARRIAGE AND THE BABY BOOM

"Oh look! What is going on?" I asked. "It appears that the majority of girls and women who are around are pregnant! And, it looks as if they have been summoned to assemble in a designated spot." (I later realized they were just waiting for public transportation). Goldteeth intervened, although reading thoughts and said, "Nowadays, we are experiencing a baby boom because there are too many people who are jobless. These people may rely on their parents or relatives for support. Often, when these people are not working and have nothing else to do, they engage in social relationships, such as having sexual intercourse as much as they want. What's more, in the past, many people followed family planning, which was necessary for the married couples. The domiciliary nurses used to visit individual family's home and go from house to house to educate them concerning family planning. They also taught them how to take care of newborns, nourishing them with the appropriate baby foods and so forth. The nursery method is still in place today. However, there are not many domiciliary nurses left, to go around from house to house. There is no one obliged to execute their duties today. Consequently, the baby's mother is prone to feed the baby with chunky homemade foods, which at times are not nourishing. This is what makes the baby underweight, fragile and feeble looking.

Goldteeth continues, sadly, "Before, the appearance of babies was not like that. Our politicians who are supposedly there to see to it that people maintain good health are doing a very poor job. Poverty is rampant, not only herein the Paradise city but throughout the nation as a whole"

Then, I pondered about the survival of the siblings and the children.

"Stop!" he exclaimed. "Many of the babies don't see their next birthday, because of malnutrition of the children. When the children are sick, their parents take them to the pediatric hospital treatment. But the trouble is that there is no effective medication to treat them. Or, there may be no medication that is appropriate to dispense, making the doctor dispense some popular native medicine."

I am anxious to find out if many of the pregnant women are married, or not. In some instances, many women at times have customary marriages and stay by their husbands. In other circumstances, some women leave their husbands and dump their children. It, therefore, becomes the responsibility of the husband to take care of the children. If the husband is a middle-class man, the children will not suffer or have malnutrition. On the other hand, a poor husband may continue to live from hand to mouth, creating poor nourishment for the kids. So, the traditional separated wife is free to seek another man to become her husband. In this case, the husband may be poor or rich. It depends on the woman's luck.

However, a lawful marriage does exist. There are the Paradise City Hall marriages and the Church or Muslim marriages. These types seem to last longer than the customary. The lawful marriage could end with a divorce when husband and wife are tired of each other. Separations were not too common as they are today. In early days, parents intervened whenever they suspected a separation. Accordingly, the husband and wife usually heeded their parents, something which is not common today. Today, most of the women are free to do whatever they want. As a result, many married and unmarried children disrespect their parents.

I asked if there is a marriage ceremony to commiserate marriages. Goldteeth explained to me that there are different kinds of ceremonies - other than Christian and Muslim. Those, however, are the major ones, which the parents admire.

For the Christian ceremony, relatives, friends and acquaintances are usually invited to the husband's house. But the gathering, seating, eating and dancing are done under the tents, purposely meant for outside ceremonies. If the ceremony is in the day, the ceremony continues until all the invitees are tired and leave. There are usually no disturbances during the ceremony. "However, the opulent Christian ceremony cannot go on today." Goldteeth declared, "The reason is that when the ceremony is going on there are many onlookers watching, the invitees begin panicking, because the onlookers may have thieves among them. The thieves are always watching the invitees and how they are spraying money on the foreheads of the hosts. Consequently, the guest must be very careful when they are ready to leave the party because the thieves will secretly follow any one of the guests whom they feel they can prey upon."

He goes on with his comparison, "On the other hand, the Muslim way is almost the same except they usually perform their ceremony in a formal mosque congregation setting whereby singing by praising Allah with dancing. Furthermore, the orthodox religious Muslims do not dance, instead they will be praying by counting the Muslim's rosary. In addition, the chief Imam with his followers as well as invitees will sit down preaching and praying for the bride and groom. As the prayer goes on, the bride or groom, relatives, acquaintances and guests will continuously put money in a special bowl which is always in front of the chief Imam. This procession will stop when the money is not put in the special bowl anymore."

# DEMOGRAPHIC ENVIRONMENT

## GREETING

Goldteeth and I stand outside in front of a renowned person's building chatting and laughing and also observing how people greet one another. At first, we want to be stationary, where both of us stood. Nevertheless, we see a couple of people chatting and laughing nearby and we developed an urgent curiosity, and want to poke our nose into why such chatting and laughing was going on.

We proceed toward the two people. As we got closer to them, they paid us no attention, as their chatting was loud. We did not disturb their conversation, but my partner pulled me on the side and said to me that the two greeted each other; yet, both fell right into amicable conversation.

When Goldteeth mentioned the word greeting, I decided to inquire further whether greeting is valued by the Paradise city inhabitants or not. Then my partner opens up to explain in detail.

"Customs are very important in our culture", Goldteeth stated, people used to greet one another whether they knew each other or not. It was out of respect, especially, if they lived in the same house or neighborhood. In fact, when area people acquainted with one another and recognized each other the person who sees the known familiar person would greet first. If the person being greeted could not hear the greeting word, the person greeting would call the person's name. When the person hears his name being called, he would look at the calling direction and would reciprocate in an appreciative manner. If the two who greeted each other had time for each other, the two people would stop and chat and would open the conversation that pertains to either each others' family or pertains to the environment they were both living in or pertains to the current news of the day. This is what these two people are doing as we are looking at them now."

"Greetings among people used to be another source of education, either directly or indirectly", Goldteeth continued. "For instance, in the past, whenever people opened a greeting, people tended to inform each other about something he forgot which might still be in existence. Or, if he had wanted to go somewhere and he did not know how to go about it, the person who is knowledgeable would give the precise information that would shed light on how to get to the actual place."

Today, according to my partner, greeting is not a big deal anymore. In other words, if a person sees someone he knows, and tries to greet him or her verbally, the other person may pretend to not hear - or he may walk faster, in order to avoid or antagonize the person. In addition, the person may also assume that the person who initiated the greeting wants something - like monetary help. This kind of behavior is very common in the city, to the extent that it opens an atmosphere of distrust between the greeter and the greeted.

Despite this type of behavior amongst the city inhabitants, people still in their hearts believe in greeting. Unfortunately, the significance which was once bestowed upon formal greeting, has now, however, almost disappeared.

# GEOGRAPHIC ENVIRONMENT

# GEOGRAPHIC ENVIRONMENT

## CITY APPEARANCE

I spoke to Billo, the lawyer, in person who said, "The Certificate of Occupancy is on the typist's desk at the COO Office. It will later be authorized by the commissioner of Land Reacquisition - with his signature and the affixed seal of Paradise City and Paradise State." He said that upon notification that it is ready to go, he would pick it up for me. "The process could be 1 month or six months. It depends on how back-logged they are. I have done all the proper paperwork. Don't worry, we are almost there."

I wondered to myself, "How long will this take now?" But, I keep myself busy by writing about the obvious corruption that has gripped Paradise City. This way, I can keep my mind off of how long everything is taking with building my house. I'm glad Goldteeth has been available to me. I am supposed to meet my pal to continue on my quest of checking the lifestyles and demise of my dreamland, Paradise City.

Upon completing the meeting with Billo, I rushed to meet him, so as not to be late. We decide to turn out first. If we get tired later, we could take public transportation.

We set out walking slowly along the sidewalk. Suddenly, we collided against four people, two of whom started cursing us out. But, we ignored the two and moved ahead. "How did we manage to collide with those four a few minutes ago?" I asked my partner.

Goldteeth said to me, "If we are not careful, it will happen again. We have to watch where we are going or we could collide with passersby. It will continue until we move away completely from the crowds."

"Why?" I inquired.

Nevertheless, "Before my partner finishes explaining, we reached a crowded area where we both had to walk sideways in order to pass through". A few yards away, we observe that one of the local streets is full of shoppers, non-shoppers and pedestrians, as well as the wheel- barrow pushers. When this pedestrian traffic comes to a complete halt, it cripples movement and people decide to just squat down where they are to mingle with the crowd. Instead of continuously forcing our way through the crowd, we manage to find out way to a less crowded side street.

While my partner is accustomed to the rough streets and at the same time we are sweating while the sun reaches its peak, I am not. So, I suggest we take a taxi cab or public transportation. He laughed at me.

"Why are you laughing?" I asked him: 'I am a little upset'.

He replied that "We are not going to get any transportation in this location, because of the heavy crowd congestion that we are stuck in. Besides, he proclaimed, that the drivers for passengers cars and commercial vehicles' parking stop is located in another part of the area. At that location, we could probably get any kind of transportation of our choice. But, even at that location, we could wait for an hour before we can get a public transportation. The reason for this is because the buses or cabs are always full with passengers. What's more, by the time we do get on it's like squeezing oranges among those who are already seated." Not something I wanted to do. But, since we weren't moving anyway, we gave it a try.

In the past, the Paradise city population was a lot less than what it is today. The shopping centers, as well as the flow of the traffic, were not this congested. Instead, the streets were relatively normal for the flow of the traffic. In fact, when people shopped they moved freely and briskly. They usually picked out their merchandise from the shelves, without this pushing and shoving one another and without being among much of the crowd.

Today, so many different nationalities migrate from other parts of the nation as well as from the neighboring nations to settle in the city of Paradise, with the hope of securing a job to take care of their families. Without providing additional accommodations, it becomes a real nightmare.

# GEOGRAPHIC ENVIRONMENT

## CITY CONDITIONS

Just as I approach my friend Goldteeth to start our walk for today, I get a call from the new contractor who says - he is running out of money. The dollar to nira today is 157 to one. The stock market for nira fell today, "So it could be 158. I will borrow money from the bank and get it to you as soon as possible", I said. "It is always costing more money," I thought to myself. But, I knew he was good and trustworthy. If he needed it, then he needed it, no matter how much I wished it to be 158 or 159 or 160.

After hanging up from my contractor, I looked at the city island lagoon. We near the BASIN section of the city of Paradise, and I noticed the nasty, yellowish colored lagoon. "Why am I buying land here?" I remembered this used to be a very picturesque, crystal-blue lagoon years back. So I'm wondering, 'Am I some kind of fool?' Out loud I query Goldteeth, "Why is the lagoon water yellowish and filthy?"

He smiled, and says to me, "Calm down Irepo. The water turned dirty, ever since the capital was relocated to Idera, the new nation's capital. Do you recall - the ferry boat – which used to transport passengers or workers to the PAPA area was in the mainland? There was a big fire and it was burnt down to the ground - and was relocated, away from where it usually docked, to a hidden area and then dumped into the lagoon. After that, all you could see was this once good-looking passenger vehicle just floating by, looking burnt-out and raggedy. It's dumping created such eye-sore for people who saw it where it was dumped."

As soon as he mentioned the dumping of the burnt boat, I spotted it where it had been dumped. Upon closer explanation, we found other rubbish dumped on it as well, about ten yards away floating in the water. I was furious! So, I asked my partner, "Why the dumping of refuse is a common behavior of the citizens?" To which he has no quick answer and neither do I.

We continued to lament about the rubbish. We also observed the lagoon was always filled with fishermen, who once caught fish there.

I asked him to explain why there are only a few fishermen on the lagoon now? He responded, "There are fewer fish left in the lagoon to catch. Thus, many fishermen are out of fishing jobs. The few that are fishing, as we speak, are struggling to catch fishes to sell locally so that they use the money to take care of their families. Other things which used to make the lagoon attractive at night including different kinds of colorful lights which illuminated the ships, boats and canoes have all disappeared. The lagoon looks dark and desolate at night, as if it was deserted and dangerous. The corrupt politicians, as well as the economic recession are the cause for the neglect.

Later, as we stroll along the streets, we noticed many old houses that need revamping, but the owners do nothing to make their layouts look beautiful. A few of the dilapidated old houses have been demolished, with no new houses built to replace them. As a result, garbage is dumped on the premises. There are some that have been rebuilt and are newly painted. Still, the paint has started peeling, making the appearance of the rebuilt houses also look dirty with faded painting. We also observed that the majority of the public lavatories are not in use. The city of Paradise has neglected them and consequently their appearances are a major eye-sore and they have been boarded up to prevent people from using them as dumping places. In addition, dirty tap water pumps are also neglected, rusty and filthy surrounded with muddy water.

Years ago, the lagoon's water used to be a beautiful blue, making its banks clean and accessible so workers could relax there during lunch hours. At night, canoes, small boats, as well as ships had colored lights which made the scenery pretty. The street's tap water pumps were in use and clean. They were frequently washed early in the morning before they were used by the public. Consequently, pedestrians walking near them would not be assaulted with the smell of stagnant water. The majority of houses and buildings were constantly updated, freshly painted and well maintained.

In conclusion, the rough appearances of the city of Paradise are due largely to negligence and corrupt practices are due largely to negligence and corrupt practices of the politicians in the city government who failed to revamp the city frequently.

# GEOGRAPHIC ENVIRONMENT

## CENSUS TIME

Goldteeth's wife has gone to visit a family member, so he is not in good sorts. He truly misses her.

In 2006, the census for the nation took place. "Oh!" Goldteeth shouted loudly, "You know, my friend, the Paradise city's counting and procedure are horrendous."

"Explain! Explain! I am anxious to hear how it goes from a person like you who never traveled abroad."

His explanation was interesting, "The census' officers, clerks and administrators are selected and dispatched to various constituencies. But they are probably not together so that some of them are confused because of constant relocation to different sites. They did not show up at where they were supposed to be sometimes - while the citizens were waiting to be counted. What was really bad about the arrangement was that a curfew had been imposed throughout the City of Paradise - to keep people in doors until in the afternoon so that everybody could be counted. They wanted to be able to catch the people at home. So, everyone felt like they were on lock down in the mornings."

He continued, "If anybody was spotted outside when the curfew is on, he or she could be arrested or beaten by police officers who were monitoring the curfew. Also, cars were on the streets picking up passengers and transporting them to designated locations during the curfew. The only cars allowed to ply the streets were the police cars and army vehicles, or emergency vehicles."

Goldteeth's analysis got worse, "The census officers never ran a smooth accounting. Sometimes people were not registered as a constituent to be counted in their own area. It was when errors or names were found that they were - then relocated to where the people's names were supposed to be. In fact, many people from different neighborhoods complained that they were omitted from the list, in their constituency where the officers were operating, despite the curfew which restricted them in houses. As a result of inconsistency, the census commissioner extended the deadline date for the census. Because of the extension of the finishing date, they changed the locations the census workers were to go to. It caused mass confusion. Imagine you are on a curfew so that the census people can come to your home and they don't show up and you are taken away from going to the market to sell your goods repeatedly. People were angry and frustrated. Thus, workers, drivers and sellers of commodities could not go out to take care of their business. They were losing money and they missed the first money of each day, usually very good money. They stayed home late, living like this until the curfew is lifted. But, when the curfew was lifted in the afternoon, there was not enough time for the business men and women to transact their businesses before it became dark. And when it was dark, robbery and holdups started. Therefore, the scariness of darkness made many people dash home as quickly as possible. When the curfew was lifted, people rushed outside like locusts screaming and shouting for relief; so that they could shop in various places immediately", my partner concluded.

The effect from the mishandled census caused a great deal or chaos and disorder. Older people remember when it was more organized, and ran smoothly. "Before," he remembered, "the census was never arranged in such a hectic manner. It was always well planned and arranged properly with no curfew affixed to it. At that time, people did not worry about when it would be finished; they worried about being robbed, beaten or arrested. Back then, citizens were always counted at their leisure at homes." He ascertained that the scenario of the census of 2006 was a mêlée.

I remembered past census taking before I traveled oversees as well. As soon as the census officer entered the house, he or she was given a chair to sit in at a table so that he or she could put the necessary papers out. Then an elder in the house was called upon to give the names of the dwellers of the house. The officer would read the list of names in the register to confirm them were still alive, or had passed on. However, in 2006, I was in Paradise during the census and could not go out during the week of the census. Transportation was inaccessible. There was nobody to pilot me around Paradise City. It had changed and become very rough. There was no accurate counting because many people complained of name omissions, despite the fact that the governor of Paradise had appealed to the citizens to be available for the counting. It was a worst type of census I ever experienced.

# GEOGRAPHIC ENVIRONMENT

## POLLUTION

We attempted to walk on some of the safer streets in Paradise and cautiously cross from one place to another hoping to avoid the many careless drivers who pay no attention to the safety rules. I point my finger at many cars and busses passing by. "Look", I shout. Suddenly a huge smoke is emitted from a bus as the passengers get off. The cloud of smoke spreads and blankets the crowd like a smoke coming from a house on fire. Others also covered their noses and started coughing. They cannot move away fast enough to avoid the smoke. They have been blinded temporarily and cannot see images ahead of them; so they bump into each other. Or, they stay in a stationary position like effigies tied to poles, until the smoke subsides.

A crowd of people walk quickly passing the spot as if a police officer is chasing them. In a few minutes, we too are walking away. A big lorry loaded with building materials passes us and erupts with thick dust - which spread over the shoppers, and the street. The dust spread so much. It obstructs our view to the extent that we cannot see the same truck ahead of us, and assume that it has parked on the roadside. Soon the dust dissipates. We realize that the truck kept going. The dust's thickness impeded our sight from seeing the lorry as a non-stopping vehicle.

Subsequently, I asked Goldteeth, "Why is it that the Paradise City Council cannot do something to prevent excessive carbon dioxide emissions from the vehicles, or pave all the streets to reduce excessive dust as well?"

First of all, he reiterated his views; corruption is the evil of improvement. It can be minimized - if the Paradise City Council expenditures are spent wisely and appropriately. He said, "Any car for bus whose engine cannot start constantly, the owner puts it on the street for transporting passengers, regardless of how bad its body is dented, the raggedness or smoke emissions. As long as the vehicle can start and move, the city doesn't care about how it looks. Beauty is not a criterion for public transportation vehicles. Consequently, the smoke emissions coming from the passing vehicles can easily spread inside the stationary vehicles which are full of passengers before they move from their loading spot. Hence, passengers inhale the carbon dioxide or dust. So, they have to cover their noises until the vehicle is ready to move away from its loading location."

Carbon dioxide emissions and dust were also problems in the early days. However, the Paradise City Council always made sure that tickets were issued to violators, scofflaws, who ran unsafe vehicles on the roads to transport paying passengers, they had to pay the stipulated fine on the ticket for the carbon dioxide. The purpose for issuing the ticket was also to remind the owners as well as the drivers to repair their vehicles and to make sure that they were free of pollution before they were put on the street for public transportation.

I remembered in the past when the Paradise City Council used to immediately makes sure streets were repaired by the city before they became unbearably hazardous roads. In addition, the city made sure raggedy streets which could damage or unbalance the car and bus alignments were fixed without much fuss. Therefore, in light of this corruption, if it could be abated and focused on genuine accountability, the budget aside set for a specific purpose could repair raggedy streets and roads would be paved in a timely fashion; in other words, as soon as possible for the smooth transport of passengers and vehicles in the city.

# GEOGRAPHIC ENVIRONMENT

## LACK OF FRESH AIR

Goldteeth and I are walking together. The sun is burning brightly and intensely down on us. He is as cool as a cucumber. I, on the other hand, am sweating constantly. The sweat is running periodically from my armpit and I and my clothes are soaked in a pool of water with my clothing on.

"Today is real hot." I complained. "Are you hot?" I asked Goldteeth. "Are there no trees along the streets where you and I can go and stand under to cool off?" I continued.

Then he laughed. "Why are you laughing?" I interrogated him.

He explained that the sun does not bother him because he has gotten used to its intensity. I quickly replied to him that I am no longer used to it and needed a shady place where I could cool off.

My partner then said, "You see the passersby keep on walking in the heat without any concern about the intensity of the sun? There are no trees along the streets that could serve as a cooling spot."

As he mentioned the word tree, I instantly looked around and realized that all the trees were hemmed down and the City of Paradise was not trying to re-grow them.

"Number one", Goldteeth replied, "Trees are not planted on the streets, and the few that are around, have no leaves on them, many of them are half dead!"

I, then, inquired from my partner - if the Paradise City Council is aware of the importance of growing trees on the streets. He responded, "I believe the council does know; they are just so conniving that they don't bother to replace the dead ones." We spotted several dying and dead trees as we walked along the street.

As we crossed from one street to the next, I saw a big tree far off in the distance. I, immediately, urged Goldteeth to walk faster toward the tree. Upon reaching the tree we let out a long sigh of joy. At last, relief from the intensity of the sun! Before I explain the beauty of having trees along the side streets, a little breeze hit us. It felt so good. My friend admitted that he enjoyed the cool breeze - himself. I laughed and said to him that now he would be able to follow my point of view on having shade trees along the city side streets.

With my partner enjoying the cool breeze under the tree, we both remained for a while - just standing still, there under the tree inhaling oxygen, which is a necessity for the body. Oxygen is also a necessity for blood to circulate through our bodies. This is the basic explanation that I finally started to share with Goldteeth. What a great example to illustrate my point as we stood there. It was easier to understand my meaning from this one simple growing tree along a side street in the City of Paradise, simple, yet so profound.

"Besides", I stated, Goldteeth, if you will recall the many times I had a handkerchief, to cover my nose as we approached the dusty streets." I continued to explain my masking actions. "The reason for this is that the type of air that people inhale here is mixed with carbon dioxide in combination with the dust. To inhale this type of air is detrimental to your health. And, to constantly breathe polluted air causes respiratory problems."

Having just finished explaining the hazards of inhaling the dust and carbon monoxide at the same time, a big trailer came rolling down the half tarred street and kicking up a lot of dust. It took twenty minutes before people could see again. As the dust subsided, I observed a handful of passersby were almost stationary, coughing hard with water running from their eyes. I called them to his attention to people coughing.

He burst into laughter, and I instantly curtailed his laughter by telling him that what he sees is no laughing matter. After all, these poor people could easily develop breathing problems if they constantly continue to inhale this dusty air instead of fresh air. The beautiful fresh air that they currently have is infinitesimal. So much more could be generated from the beautiful green leaves of trees. This is an exchange between plants and humans. The plants clean the air of harmful particles and render the air sweet and aromatic.

The intensity of the sun is now pounding down on us and there is no fresh air and no place to cool off. We see passersby covering their heads with umbrellas to prevent the sun's intensity.

Eventually it is obvious that we could not use umbrellas to thwart the hot sun. There was no fresh breeze! I was sweating like a bottle of water stored in a freezer after being removed and placed on a table. The people, who are on the streets, from day to day, from moment to moment face these harsh conditions.

"The sun is up at dawn," Goldteeth declared, and does not let up until the sun goes down at night!

Later, I informed my partner that in the past - there were plenty of beautiful trees on practically every street or road - except for commercial areas. At that time, passersby didn't suffer from the sun's intensity because the trees served as a cool off spot. When people were tired and wanted to recuperate under the trees or to enjoy the fresh air they would sit and enjoy. The hazards of breathing in carbon dioxide or dust were not a problem as it is today.

In some streets where there were plenty of trees, people played cards, or engaged in telling amicable tales. Or, at times, people dozed off and even slept on the benches. If a person stopped under the trees to rest for a while, he could easily hear the sound of snoring from others. Goldteeth whispered that he concurred with my concern. He said, "The trees along the side streets used to add beauty to the structure of the City of Paradise and give the atmosphere a breath of fresh air." I was alarmed, Goldteeth seemed to gasp.

# GEOGRAPHIC ENVIRONMENT

## THE ISLANDS WITH THE BIGGEST ISLAND

The Paradise city is composed of three islands: Paradise city, Koyi Island and Victoire Island. However, the biggest island is Paradise city; while Papa, Yiba, Suruere, Shodi and Mush, etc. are not part of the islands.

Goldteeth, I would like you to tell me what you know about each one. He then decided to delineate the biggest one first.

## PARADISE CITY

Goldteeth had much to say about Paradise City, which used to be the residential centers and commercial hub for banking, petty traders and many merchants. "For decades it was the capital of Hope before they moved it to Idera. Commercial activities were plentiful. There was a lot of congestion, with the loading, unloading and repacking of goods coming from abroad, as well as from the interior part of the nation. In those days, white and blue collar workers usually got up early in the morning to avoid traffic, so that they would not be late to work. They worked for 8 hour days. They would do overtime, or hang around after work hours to play with their friends late in the evening without worrying about returning home, or the fear of being attacked by the robbers. Many trucks constantly drove through the commercial areas delivering merchandise all night, because there were workers for day and night shifts. There were no thieves to tailgate the workers, when they went home after work hours. As a result, the biggest island was like the city that did not sleep. In fact, the newspaper vendors were usually on the streets around 5am promoting and selling their papers from those early birds or those who finished work in the morning."

Paradise was once a peaceful residential area which has no resemblance to how it is today. It is filthier, overcrowded and congested. It has raggedy, neglected roads. Because of the relocation of the capital to a far away location, most of the commercial activities and merchants moved out of the city or out of business. The city was left in the hands of managers who now control the commercial activities. Most of the owners failed to train their relatives to take care of their businesses after they retire or get old, or what to do when uncontrollable incidents occurred. As a result, the island now only has a handful of industries left. Prosperous commercial shops and well-established merchants are rare. Today only a myriad of petty traders remain who have turned the island into human traffic congestion.

Finally, even though Paradise City is almost de- commercialized, the difference between then and now is that area is not patronized regularly. There is little work for both day and night work shifts, because thieves, kidnapping and killing which constantly occurred in the area. Also corruption was rampant and either directly or indirectly prevented the genuine commercialization of the city.

## VICTOIRE ISLAND

The next principal island, Victoire Island, used to have a wooden bridge which connected it to the biggest island. Later, the bridge was replaced with a concrete one.

Victoire Island used to be swampy and crab lovers used to catch different breeds of crabs to eat or sell. Later, the island was revamped and became a residential area with beautiful homes, commercial stores and shops, which sold accessories. The nationally renowned radio station was there. There were many important hotels there; the Nation Mint building was there, law schools where the pre-lawyers studied law abroad went there first to learn the nation's law and constitution before they could be allowed to practice law in the country. In addition, each individual state house erected and beautiful structures are there.

The changes which took place when Paradise City was no longer the nation's capital also affected Victoire, as well. Despite the changes that almost destroyed the beauty of the island, those individual state houses are still there. But the buildings are not well maintained. Their surroundings' facades are disgusting, the gutters are not cleaned regularly, and mildew can be seen on the structures. There are potholes on few raggedy roads. The area is not properly zoned because the commercial settings are not properly distinguished from the residential areas. Both are inter-mingled to the extent that pedestrians crossing the streets have to be extra careful.

Victoire Island has become neglected since Idera became the capitol. The federal government owns the majority of the State Houses there and has allowed them to mildew just because Paradise is no longer Capital and the government is no longer care. The Paradise City Council says there is no money to return the area back to its once beautiful luster.

The sad fact is that the island is not as attractive as it used to be. Caretakers can't afford to revamp some of the island's beautiful features so they become eye-sores. Money appropriated to improve the area is not used for what it is appropriated for. Instead, nearly half of the money is diverted into the pockets of the politicians who are reaping from the corruption in Paradise City as a whole.

## **KOYI ISLAND**

The last island which is part of the big three is the Koyi Island, which used to be an exclusive residential area for the colonial masters, before the nation acquired independence. At that time, the houses were built to suit their comfort and were carefully and constantly maintained timely. Above all, the area was completely excluded from industrial or commercial activities and other disturbances. Any unauthorized visitor who happened to be driving around trying to find a particular address would suddenly find the police by their car. The police would pull that driver over to the sidewalk to interrogate them. Otherwise, it turn out that the drivers are just trespassing the streets, the police would immediately chase the trespasser out.

However, the area is completely different today. Indigenous people occupy the residential houses since the nation won their independence. The area is deteriorated now, overcrowded with bad drainage. The streets are neglected. The island now has unregulated traffic. Thus, many of the properties' values have depreciated in comparison to when colonial masters were living there. The Paradise City Council does not maintain the area. Consequently, since the capital shifted to Idera, there has been a change of focus and priority. Also, political corruption adds to the problem, politicians are not reliable or trustworthy in handling the appropriated money to improve the area.

Obalemi, which is connected to the Koyi Island, used to be where the horses were stabled as well as an army barracks. Here, the Muslims used to worship on Fridays and on the day of Ed Fatil, an annual festivity. This area was not considered as quiet because residents had children who played there. In other areas, the children were not allowed to play outside without being attended by the house attendant or by their parents.

Nowadays, both areas are full of natives and non-natives. Obalemi once had a mix of residents who were very friendly. Unlike now that the residents do not care as much for one another. Tribalism has had a negative impact among the residents. The horse stables which used to be fascinating to tourists are no longer around. The army barracks which used to be there that served as a haven for passersby was no longer there. So, the removal of the barracks makes the area unsafe for the passersby after dark.

What's more, people cannot walk safely around anyhow at night or work late in the evenings without being escorted home because of the constant threat of robbery. Obalemi is filthier than Koyi.

# SUGGESTIONS

## TRANSPARENT ACCOUNTABILITY: A PATH TO ABATE CORRUPTION

Although there is no clear cut method alone that will minimize, prevent or wipe out corruption other than each individual citizen adapts the mindset and the determination to stop it in their own lives. There are several ways we can begin to minimize corruption within the Paradise City Council.

First of all, the Paradise City Council has to seriously impose transparent accountability from each and every individual council member, officer or designated person who holds an office of responsibility. Each individual must be held accountable for how he or she acts and be accountable for the work they are assigned to do.

To accomplish this, the Paradise City Council has to input all official council business transactions, budgeting, and projects into the city's website. This way all the city departments can see the data, review the information and proposals before they are implemented. This also allows for public scrutiny as well, so citizens are apprised of official activity.

Then, there must be an appropriate response to any criticisms or concerns before implementation can be approved. Following that, the development and progress of any projects that involve capital expenditures must be detailed on the city's website. Upon completion of the project, before it is approved as complete, there must be a careful and thorough final accounting. It should be thoroughly examined by diversified personnel before it is completely accepted. There must be a rotation of the review board every 2 or 3 years that reviews and approves projects and budgets. Bid packages for any project must be reviewed and approved by an expert reviewer before the bidding is announced.

When money is set aside for any kind of project, the source and purpose amount should be revealed immediately through the city's internal email system along with the analysis to all city departments. This way the Paradise City Council's appropriated money could be monitored openly. And most of all, it will prevent the secret spending that is now going on. The amount allocated for expenditures should not be different from what the original money was set aside for. This will prevent siphoning money to special interests.

This procedure would also enable each department to have the ability to make changes, deny it, or accept it before the appropriated money is dispersed and spent. This idea would stimulate the Paradise city officials to discuss their views on it in the open.

In addition, each project must be inspected before a project is approved and started. The inspector should be a capable inspector. By doing this, the council will not be able to hold a grudge against the hardworking inspectors for projects that are tainted. When foul play is suspected, the efficient inspector will look for where errors are. This will be punishable by law, when unwarranted mistakes are detected.

The Paradise City Council has created a vicious web of corruption pitting the 'haves' against the 'have-nots'. There is an enormously wide gap between the rich and the poor. The Paradise City Council creates a hostile environment by being comprised of so many corrupted officers, who just sit back and take bribes, and close their eyes to the injustices to the populace, particularly the poor.

The feasible way to bridge the gap between the "haves and have-nots" would be to mandate a regressive taxation for the poor people and a progressive taxation for the wealthy people. In other words, simply put: 'the less you have – the less you have to pay and the more you have – the more you have to pay. The percentages should be smaller for the poor and higher for the rich. And it should be mandated by the Paradise City Council. A specific percent should be determined and monitored. Monitoring should be on-going. This sounds right and natural. This would make the rich truly altruistic. However, the greedy rich seem not to think so.

Although, many seem to agree that the wealthy are supposed to invest some of their wealth in job creation, the majority of wealthy people in Paradise City turn their backs on the poor. They lavish their money on themselves. They have disdain and selfish attitudes toward the poor people. So, by imposing the two methods of taxation, the Paradise City Council would be required to closely monitor this taxation. It would be most effective and easier to monitor. They can have a computer application developed that would reveal the total tax nira collected.

Hence, when the Paradise City Council is proposing any expenditure, budget or project of any kind the members and the cohorts would then be aware that each proposal will be input and posted on the Paradise City Council website for everyone to see. So, when internal audits are conducted for Paradise City Council departments, there will be no discrepancies. There will be no critiques to grudge about. And if there is a discrepancy, the Paradise City council Chairman, Officials of the Paradise City Council would already be familiar with the source of the discrepancy immediately, without the finger pointing of the past with everyone blaming the other guy, no one stepping up to the plate and no one letting the buck stop with themselves. Immediate prosecution will be initiated without much ado. Consequently, the money appropriated for any project in the future would be well spent correctly and wisely. And may I add that every city in every country of Africa should adopt these policies, not just Hope. Finally, we should be mindful of Kofi Anan's statement on corruption, the former United Nations Secretary General who said, "Corruption deprives the poor from benefiting from some business activities or assistance and drains enormous amounts of money from the legitimate economy." It's simple and clear.

# CONCLUSION

The one thing I learned about doing business in Paradise City is you have to check, double check and then recheck your information - and the people you are doing business with.

My friend Goldteeth was not feeling well, so I went to his house to visit him. His wife did not greet me at the door. My associate stood there bent over in pain. He was visibly quite ill. We walked back to his bedroom where he fell into the bed. He told me his wife and son had left him, and he couldn't know their whereabouts. I offered him my condolence, advised him not to be discouraged, but to be courageous. Then, I prayed for him that God Almighty would give him moral energy to overcome his predicament.

## **HEALTH AND HYGIENE**

Paradise City Council must make health and hygiene a priority for the entire city! The price of the 'falling sick' is higher than the price of treatment. In other words, prevention is always better than trying to find a cure. As a result, wellness will minimize the astronomical cost that the sick person has to pay for treatment, especially one who has no insurance to cover doctor bills.

There should be wellness programs to help you get back to good health and hygiene. The government used to send a health care staff, such as nurses to visit families to make sure that people were maintaining their health. Without a comprehensive wellness plan, the people will just continue to fall sick and will not have a long life.

It is very simple: in order to have good health, people need to ingest uncontaminated food, true clean water and live in a hygienic environment with fresh air to breathe. There must be a stop to the illegal dispensing of illegal medicines. Medicines should be inspected for efficiency and expiration date. Good Hygiene leads to good health. Corruption at times prevents good hygiene and good health to be maintained because any government money set aside to improve on health is mostly not spent on wellness of the populace, but on intangible consumptions and others to pocket the rest of the money.

## POLITICS AND CORRUPTION

Every project or business that comes from the Paradise City Council must be monitored by an independent third party before anything is implemented. Any deviations and any extra or late ideas should be reviewed. In addition, contractors should always be held accountable for the unfinished work assigned them and they should also be ready to announce the reason why the work is unfinished. Also, the time to complete each project should be announced openly before the project started.

Corruption should be frowned upon as demoralizing behavior. Embezzlement of any of the budgeted money, corruption, conflict of interest, should be addressed and sanctioned. An example must be made of those who practice corruption so that the intelligence of the people or the project itself is not insulted or ignored. Corruption unaddressed proliferates – and our young people emulate what they see.

Leaders should refrain from using sneaky, deceptive practices. Corruption money that powerful people acquire directly or indirectly has to be transformed. Corruption has created the economic recession that we experience today. Leaders must find a way to stimulate economic stability rather than focusing on dodging the problem because it turns into an uncontrollable unemployment situation. It should be the concern of every citizen to desist from corruption. This behavior must be abated. However, the government needs to let education be the most concentrated means of reducing the high intensity of corruption that is spreading like venereal disease in Paradise City. The men and youngsters should be encouraged to go to school to upgrade their minds toward economic improvement; whereby they would be self sufficient, aware of the evil effects of corruption. Not only going to school to acquire more knowledge but also the government should make use of radio, television to announce that corruption of any form would not be tolerated and anybody caught would be prosecuted with heavy fines or jailed without parole.

## TRANSPORTATION, POLICE AND CORRUPTION

The transportation system in the Paradise city is an eye-sore. Transportation must be maintained and controlled properly. A study should be made of other transportation systems to see what can be adopted for Paradise.

Although, a few drivers attempt to prevent accidents, there are so many bad drivers who choose not to yield to the traffic regulations. Pedestrians are not always safe when walking on the road or crossing the street. Sidewalks and crosswalks should be a safe distance from the streets.

Some police pretend to control traffic situations and even pretend to arrest traffic offenders, while actually they are engaging in a bribe. The police should be given the necessary tools, to go after the scofflaws who constantly violate the traffic laws. The police should be given better salaries. The aim should be to curb the violators and to encourage police to control and maintain traffic.

## WATER SYSTEM

Paradise City should have a reservoir - so that the city will have clean drinkable tap water. Paradise City should not have to rely on the so called dug-hole well. To say there is no money to maintain clean drinking water, is a flimsy excuse. Modern new technology can even sanitize well water.

The 'dug-hole wells' are rampant throughout the entire city, as well as many other parts of the nation. This reminds us of a rudimentary time before economic development, (years back), the starting point when we tried to obtain contaminated-free water to drink. Just recently every household in the city used to enjoy clean tap water as did business, municipal buildings and hospitals. Water was available all the time. What happened? The Paradise city must go back and dredge out the reservoir or build a new one as quickly as possible. Otherwise, the city will revert to old rural methods.

## ELECTRICITY

Paradise City should enjoy electrical services every day. Before, the city used constant electrical service added to the infrastructural and industrial development. Industries were prospering. But, then, all the old power plants were dismantled and replaced with new ones. We urge the city to go back to electricity usage. Furthermore, the political lobbyists should be disregarded. In other words, they should not be allowed to use their political influences to control electricity outage franchise. Only the company bided to man electricity should control the flow of electricity and it should be held responsible for its lighting and maintenance always.

## EDUCATION

The valued students are now assuming that graduation is not necessary. The value of education has deteriorated tremendously. There are no adequate supplies for school children. School teachers are not teaching on grade level and should be teaching above par, to meet the challenges that are awaiting our youth. The school buildings are unattractive for learning. There should be high quality learning, so that the pupils will be proud of themselves when they leave school. When they go home or elsewhere their demonstration of their learning should be viewed as an achievement. Children are going to school without learning much based on their report, according to my pal. Many would not be competitive when they finish. However, many choose to cut classes as their parents tried to encourage them by force, that "money talks". They focus on how they would get quick money to spend for their needs. Even though many of the parents are poor, still they give them money that they could afford, yet education is not a priority to them. It seems that, later on, they would realize that education would always be a stimulus for economic development. Also, it would make them grow in knowledge and become the leaders of tomorrow.

## HOUSING AND HEALTH

Many people in Paradise abide in substandard housing. The filthy surroundings, in addition to the dilapidated condition of many homes create a detriment to a healthy lifestyle. If people do not live in hygienic surroundings, their life span is shortened. Paradise City Council should encourage the inhabitants to be aware that good housing and clean surroundings are conducive to a longer life span. It is our belief that the Paradise City Council has the money. If embezzlement is put aside, and if corruption is minimized at the lease, while homes were renovated instead just residing in the City of Paradise, Paradise City would be comfortable and free from contagious disease.

## SUMMATION BY GOLDTEETH

Goldteeth says, "Corruption derives from corrupt people. Corruption is widespread among politicians." "Corruption could be averted by electing an independent auditor, someone from another council, not the same city, to curtail corrupt practices. The budget must be monitored to prevent over budgeting for expenditures which equals overspending and pilfering. "This money ends up in the hands of perpetrators rather than going to a good cause. This is part of what triggers inflation, recession and a higher cost of living."

Money should be sent aside to repair and maintain infrastructure such as new buildings and renovations. This money should be available for preventative measures, emergencies and for future use. Paradise City Council should not wait until the streets or roads and other problems become eye sores. They must repair them as soon as they begin to deteriorate.

## SUMMARY

It is time for me to go back to the United States. My wife misses me and I have much business to attend to. I have boarded the plane at Murila International Airport. Before leaving, the lawyer told me it was just a waiting game for the Certificate of Occupancy to be graced with a signature and the official seal. So, I signed an affidavit with him to collect the COO. I am still waiting for him to call me and let me know it has been issued and collected.

After my lawyer had assured getting the COO for me, Goldteeth and I ended our conversation on the Cycle of Corruption. I shook his hand, thanked him for being sincere with his answers given; when questions were posed to him. So I gave him money to show my appreciation - for all his relentless support that he had offered.

The deterioration of the City of Paradise is still multiplying like a venereal disease. It is clear that disorderliness and lewdness of the city is the result of neglect and corruption.

Paradise City looks as if it could never be revamped. The politicians are refusing to make it look better and modern. Therefore, we are calling on present and future council members, to revamp the city in a healthy and modern way. We want out citizens, migrants, immigrants and visitors to feel good, safe and proud to visit or reside in the City of Paradise.

I am airborne now. I am waving farewell to my Paradise City, my dreamland and thinking, 'Until we meet again.'